Rebecca Matcoff

PATHWAYS THROUGH THE HOLOCAUST

An Oral History by Eye-Witnesses

PATHWAYS THROUGH THE HOLOCAUST

An Oral History by Eye-Witnesses

by

CLARA ISAACMAN

illustrated by

Janet Katz

KTAV PUBLISHING HOUSE, INC.

in loving memory of my
"Yiddishe Mama"
Rose Heller
the most beautiful rose
I ever knew.

NBP-90
COPYRIGHT© 1988
KTAV PUBLISHING HOUSE, INC.
ISBN 0-88125-268-9

TABLE OF CONTENTS

Acknowledgements

I am indebted to many people who were helpful to me in preparation of the book *Pathways Through the Holocaust*.

First, thanks to Dr. Howard Adelman, who formulated the original premise of the book, carefully checked each chapter, suggested additions and deletions, and supervised the preparation of the text from the beginning to the very end. He was a constant source of encouragement throughout my work on the project.

I am grateful to Robert Milch for the two introductory chapters, ''The Jews of Europe'' and ''Nazis and the Holocaust.'' His scholarly approach has added historical background and deep understanding to the root causes of the Holocaust.

Much thanks to Rabbi David Sofian for the ethical teaching units at the end of each chapter. He offers a variety of constructive exercises, techniques, and moral dilemmas related to the Holocaust. These ''foundation stone'' teaching units will bring the lessons of the Holocaust to the forefront.

Thanks to Rabbi Joel Alpert of Knesseth Israel for his encouragement and support in writing this book.

Tamar Katz, Marilyn Smith, Judy Rosenstein, and Daniel C. Cohen also helped.

Professor Nora Levin, the Director of the Gratz College Holocaust Archives, was also on call.

I wish to express my gratitude to Mr. Klaus Heck for permission to condense the story, ''Before You Cast the First Stone.'' The story now appears as Innocence.

My thanks also to Mr. Errikos Sevillias for permission to condense the book, *Athens - Auschwitz*. The story now appears as Darkness in the Synagogue.

Preface

In your lifetime you will probably read many books and stories about people and events happening in the world. By now you are familiar with some based on real life, and some not. No doubt you have also heard from family and friends about events in their lives. What we hear, read, see or feel is not always easy to understand and explain. However, in this book, the stories that are being told to you now have not been told for a long time or very often. This is because the people telling the stories did not want to relive their pain and so kept silent for such a long time.

These are true stories that you will be reading, told by Holocaust survivors. They are telling what they remember. Some of their experiences were so horrible that they have blocked them out of their memories, because, as they remembered, there came a disbelief that they truly had lived through that unbelievable time. Having miraculously survived the Holocaust, these survivors came to America dreaming of starting a new life and trying to forget the past. Try as they might, they couldn't forget, as their values in life had changed forever. Therefore, they are now telling you what they can bear to remember, hoping that as you read these stories you will do so with a strong desire to understand what happened to them in the Holocaust.

It was not so long ago, because many of your relatives were alive when the Holocaust happened, and perhaps some fought in World War II, or suffered during the Holocaust. It did not happen in the days of the Pharaoh, so to help you understand these stories this collection begins with a historical overview of the events which led up to the Holocaust. This history is important to understand for seeing why people did what they did.

Each story is followed by a series of questions and materials from Jewish tradition to help you understand the real tensions involved when people living in trying times must make decisions which affect their lives and the well-being of others.

This book was created and the stories were collected and prepared by a Holocaust survivor, Clara Isaacman. She suffered through the Holocaust and now teaches in Jewish and non-Jewish schools in the Philadelphia area.

Her own Holocaust experiences, *Clara's Story*, was recently published.

The Jews of Europe

Jews first settled in Europe more than 2,000 years ago. In the time of Julius Caesar, around 50 B.C. E., there was already a large Jewish community in the city of Rome. Under the Roman Empire, which ruled most of western and southeastern Europe, Jews began to live in many other areas. They settled in Roman provinces that later became Italy, Spain, France, Germany and eventually Austria, Hungary and Czechoslovakia. They were welcomed in these countries because they had valuable skills in business, commerce and crafts. Before long they began to feel at home in their new countries.

Synagogue in Rome, fifth century C.E. (Note the Eternal Light.)

However, the peoples of Europe, who were mostly Christians, developed hostile feelings towards their Jewish neighbors. The Christians believed that Jesus was their Savior. They were taught that the Jews, by remaining Jews rather than becoming Christians, rejected Jesus.

In the Middle Ages

During the Middle Ages, these hostile Christian attitudes led to outbreaks of anti-Jewish violence. Sometimes, especially during the Crusades, mobs attacked Jewish communities, burning, robbing and killing. In some places, such as England and France, entire Jewish communities were forced to leave their homes and businesses and move to other countries. Throughout Europe at one time or another, Jews were forced to obey discriminatory laws. They were not permitted to engage in the same occupations as Christians, and had to pay special taxes and wear distinctive clothing which

Kneeling Jews reciting the humiliating *"More Judaica,"* the Jew's Oath, before a Christian judge in Augsburg, Germany, 1509.

9

would identify them as Jews. Copies of the Talmud and other Jewish holy books were confiscated and publicly destroyed and burned.

Many Jews from Germany began to settle in eastern Europe. They settled in Poland, where such cities as Vilna and Warsaw were becoming major political and economic centers. There they continued to speak the German language. In time this version of German evolved into the distinctive Jewish language known as Yiddish.

The Jews had been invited to Poland by the king because of their valuable commercial, administrative, and crafts skills, but there was much Christian hostility against them. Over the years, the Jewish communities of Poland spread into the Ukraine and Lithuania, which at the time were ruled by Poland. As the Polish Jewish communities grew and prospered, resentment and jealousy increased.

Meanwhile, anti-Jewish attitudes persisted in western Europe as well. In 1492, the same year that Columbus discovered America, the large and prosperous Jewish community of Spain was expelled. Some Spanish Jews found new homes in Holland, Italy, or even in America. Most of them, however, went to Greece, Bulgaria, and other parts of the Turkish Empire, whose ruler, the sultan, like the king of Poland earlier, had invited them because of their valuable skills. In time the Greek city of Salonika became one of Europe's major Jewish centers.

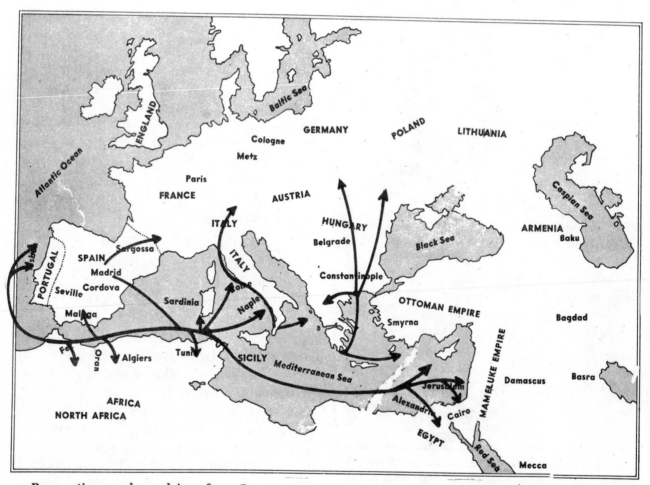

Persecutions and expulsions from German states (1350–1648). The many expulsions sent Jews eastward to Poland, where they were welcomed, and where they helped build up industry and trade.

A scene in a Spanish synagogue, from the *Sarajevo Haggadah*.

Elsewhere in western Europe anti-Jewish feeling also continued to flare up. In 1516, the city-state of Venice, in Italy, forced its Jews to live in a walled-in, restricted area known as the Ghetto. Before long the Jews of many other European cities were also forced to live in ghettos.

Despite the hostility against them, the Jews of Europe prospered. Living in their own communities, they cherished their Jewish customs and culture, leading proud and happy lives. Although Christians often treated them shamefully, Jewish scholarship and religion flourished. A vibrant and constructive existence went on within Europe's ghettos: the traditional laws of Judaism were taught, synagogues and study houses were the center of life, and the dream of someday returning to the land of Israel provided encouragement and hope.

The Age of Enlightenment

As the Middle Ages came to an end, the countries of western Europe entered the period known as the Enlightenment. New ideas of tolerance and of open-mindedness toward people who were different began to spread. Although many Christian Europeans still disliked the Jews, the ghetto gates were partially opened. The Jews of western Europe were given some opportunities to participate in European life, with some political rights. However, the reluctance to grant them full equality became known as the "Jewish Question."

The ideas of the Enlightenment had little effect in eastern Europe, where the Jews of the Ukraine, Lithuania, and most of Poland were all now under the rule of the Russian Empire, but they transformed Jewish life in western Europe. The Jews, with their ingenuity, brainpower, and energy, had long been locked within the ghetto walls. Now

Gate leading to the Jewish ghetto at Vienna.

11

Moses Mendelssohn, cultural leader in Berlin in the eighteenth century, who wished to educate his fellow Jews so that they might be accepted as German citizens.

they burst out into almost all areas of society. Never before had Jews achieved such great things in so many different fields—business, finance, literature, art, music, science, government, and education.

These achievements made some Jews feel more at home in Europe. Many of them began to think of themselves as Germans, Hungarians, or Frenchmen first, and as Jews second. Seeing themselves as no different from their non-Jewish fellow citizens in any way except religion, they began making changes in Jewish practice and worship so that Judaism would seem more similar to the religion of their countrymen.

In Germany, around the middle of the nineteenth century, these changes led to the beginning of what is now called Reform Judaism, and somewhat later to what is now called Conservative Judaism. Large numbers of German Jews adhered to the traditional understanding of the Jewish religious heritage, now called Orthodox Judaism. Many others, however, were attracted by the new religious trends. In eastern Europe, though, Hasidism won numerous followers.

While some Christian Europeans were willing to accept the Jews as fellow citizens, many others resented their successes. The old religious prejudices against the Jews had never died out, even during the Enlightenment. Now they were reinforced by a new kind of anti-Jewish hostility.

In Europe social and political change was disturbing to some people because it upset the usual way of thinking or doing things. Many people opposed modern ideas and even democracy itself. Using Jew-hatred as their weapon, some opponents of change accused the Jews of causing the problems brought about by the new social and political developments.

Attacks of this kind were often fortified by claims that the Jews were "foreigners." As non-European "Semites," they could not contribute to western culture, and would never be integrated into the "host" peoples among whom they lived, even if they abandoned Judaism.

A Hasidic rabbi giving his blessings to a young follower, about 1815.

The totally false claim that the Jews belonged to a "Semitic" race led to the origin of the term "anti-Semitism" to designate prejudice against Jews as a people rather than as just members of another religious group. By the late nineteenth century, political and racial anti-Semitism was gaining wide acceptance, especially in Germany, the home of western Europe's largest Jewish community.

In Germany and other countries, some politicians used anti-Semitism as a way to win votes. Combined with appeals to patriotism and "scientific" claims about race, this helped to make anti-Semitism "respectable."

Despite the rise of anti-Semitism, many people in Europe had a strong belief in progress. Thanks to the many new developments in science and industry, life in general seemed to be improving, and continued improvement was expected in the future. Soon, it was felt, people would solve the most serious economic and social problems, and when this happened, prejudice and political conflict would come to an end.

Fully accepting this idea, many Jews believed that the prejudice against them was bound to disappear. In Germany and elsewhere in western Europe, they confidently looked forward to a steady improvement in their situation. Eager to demonstrate that the things the anti-Semites said about them were untrue, they tried in every way to be good citizens—patriotic, law-abiding, cultured—and were certain that someday they would be fully accepted.

The Jews of Europe

Something to Think About

In the section you just read, you learned how the Jews spread out through the Roman Empire and then some of what happened to them. Unfortunately, as time passed negative attitudes developed towards Jews. Because these attitudes of hatred have persisted even to our own time, it is worthwhile for you to think about them. Does our heritage teach us anything about this? What did the Rabbis say about gentiles who have negative attitudes towards Jews? And what did they say about the Jewish suffering that resulted?

Voices from Tradition

"My hand lays hold on judgment, I will inflict punishment on My foes" (Deuteronomy 32:41)....But does the hand return empty? No, for it says, "I will inflict punishment on My foes, and I will recompense them that hate me." And who are these? The nations of the world.

— Mekilta (Shirata 4)

"Thou hast dove's eyes." (Song of Songs 1:15). As the dove is virtuous, so the Israelites are virtuous. As the dove stretches out her neck to the slaughterer, so do the Israelites, for it is said, "For Your sake are we killed all the day long" (Psalms 44:23). As the dove atones for sins, so the Israelites atone for the nations, for the seventy oxen which they offer on the festivals represent the seventy peoples, so that the world may not be depopulated of them; as it says, "In return for My love they are to become My enemies, but I pray" (Psalms 104:4). As the dove, from the hour when she recognizes her mate, does not change him, so the Israelites, from the time when they recognize the Holy One, have not changed Him.

— Song of Songs Rabbah I

Even when, for their sins, God slays Israel in this world, there is healing for them in the world-to-come, as it is said, "Come, let us return unto the Lord, for it is He who has torn us, and He will bind us up; after two days He will revive us; on the third day He will raise us up" (Hosea 6:2). The two days are this world and the days of the Messiah; the third day is the world-to-come.

— Tanna de-vei Eliahu 29

14

And in Your Opinion...

A separate point of view is expressed in each of the rabbinic passages above with which you may or may not agree. In the Mekilta passage we find a very simple and direct response to those who have hurt the Jewish people: eventually God will even the score for hurting us (God's people). In the Midrash from Song of Songs Rabbah we see a very different kind of reaction. Here the Jewish people is likened to a sacrificial dove. Just as the sacrifice of a dove atoned for the sins of the person who sacrificed it (the Jewish people), the sacrifice of Jews atones for the nations who hurt them. The third passage, from Tanna de-vei Eliahu, has a different point of view altogether. Here the suffering of the Jews at the hand of gentiles is understood as God's punishment for Jewish sins in this world, leaving only reward for Jews in the world-to-come.

So three very different rabbinic ideas are expressed responding to the persecution and suffering of Jews at the hands of gentiles. With which idea do you most agree? Do you think God will eventually punish those who hurt God's people, the Jewish people? Do you think it is somehow part of God's plan that Jews suffer to make atonement for others? Do you think Jews suffer because of our own sins, and that ultimately God will reward us for our righteousness? Since the material above is rabbinic, the answers given are all theological. Maybe you don't agree with any of these points of view, preferring some other kind of answer. Maybe you agree that a theological answer is necessary but don't agree with any of the answers above. If so, how do you answer the question of why the Jewish people (God's chosen people) has suffered at the hands of gentiles?

Nazis and the Holocaust

Perhaps all of this would have come about, but in 1914 World War I began. This great conflict set in motion a chain of events that ended more than two decades later in the Holocaust, a disaster for the Jews, and indeed for the whole world, unlike anything that had ever happened before in human history.

Germany was defeated in World War I after a four-year struggle that left its people exhausted and divided. The harsh peace terms of the Versailles Treaty imposed by the victorious French and British, who ignored the more moderate policies suggested by President Woodrow Wilson, placed a heavy economic burden on them.

Before the war Germany had thought of itself as Europe's greatest nation. Now it was confused, bitter, and economically crippled, its wealth drained to pay the vast sums demanded by the Versailles Peace Treaty.

The Rise of Hitler

As rising inflation left many Germans poor and others jobless, political differences exploded in assassinations and street fighting. Germany's new government, the

Jewish delegates to the Versailles Peace Conference.

Weimar Republic, was democratic, but its inability to prevent disorder made many people lose faith in democracy. With Germans of all outlooks desperately seeking solutions for the nation's problems, Adolf Hitler and the Nazi Party began their climb to power.

Hitler was born in 1889 in Austria. A frustrated artist who thought of himself as having great talent and was bitter because no one else agreed, he spent his early life in Vienna, the Austrian capital, and served as a corporal in the German army during World War I.

After the war Hitler became active in politics. Dominated by hatred for the Jews and by the belief that the Aryan (German) "race" was superior to all other peoples, Hitler was gifted with effective political talents. He offered an explanation for Germany's defeat, and a vision of Germany's future destiny, that played upon the fears, prejudices, and hopes of many Germans. He promised to rebuild Germany's power and restore its prosperity.

At first Hitler met with setbacks, including a short term in prison after he tried to take over the state government of Bavaria in 1923. Before long, however, he and the Nazi Party were winning large numbers of supporters. Some of them were attracted by Hitler's personality or by the Nazi program. Others disliked him and did not find his ideas convincing, but had their own reasons for backing him. Factory owners, for example, hoped that business would improve under Hitler's rule. Many of the unemployed felt that he would provide jobs.

In 1933, although the Nazis did not receive a majority of the votes, Hitler became Chancellor. He soon set about establishing the most brutal dictatorship the world had ever known.

Anti-Semitism had always played a role in Nazi propaganda, for Hitler blamed most of Germany's troubles on the Jews. Now he began putting his anti-Semitic ideas into effect.

On April 1, 1933, the Nazis sponsored Boycott Day, during which "good" Germans were not to shop in Jewish stores. The sign on the store in the photograph reads: "Germans! Defend Yourselves! Do not buy from Jews."

Anti-Jewish laws of every kind were passed. Jews could no longer be judges, lawyers, teachers, government officials, army officers. Jewish doctors could not treat non-Jewish patients, Jews could not employ non-Jews, Jews and non-Jews could not have friendly social relationships. Jewish property was taken by the government, Jewish businesses were closed down, Jewish children could not attend public schools.

Radio, movies, newspapers—all the media of communications—were utilized to spread anti-Jewish messages. On the street Jews were mocked, tormented, and even beaten. Forced to wear Star of David armbands, Jews were often attacked by Nazi storm-troopers when they ventured out. On November 9–10, 1938, known in German as Kristallnacht ("Night of the Broken Glass"), hundreds of synagogues throughout Germany were burned by Nazi mobs.

Most German Jews loved Germany and contributed to its outstanding cultural achievements. Many of them refused to leave the country when leaving was still possible. They were sure their fellow Germans would eventually turn against Hitler and the Nazis.

The Search for Refuge

Thousands of other Jews, however, fled from Germany to find refuge in other countries. Thousands more would have done so but couldn't, mainly because it was hard to find a place to go to.

Outside Germany, few people cared much about what was happening there, and many felt it was none of their business. They were troubled by problems in their own countries. With millions of workers unemployed because of the Great Depression, it was feared that German Jews would compete for the few remaining jobs.

Kristallnacht was an anti-Jewish pogrom on November 9–10, 1938. Jewish property, businesses, and synagogues were attacked and burned by Nazi mobs. This night of horror became known as "Kristallnacht" ("night of the broken glass") because so many thousands of Jewish windows were smashed.

Anti-Nazi demonstration in New York City on May 10, 1933.

Thus the countries of Europe, and the United States too, only admitted small numbers of Jews. Moreover, those Jews who managed to gain admission to a new country experienced many difficulties along the way. The immigration process was often controlled by officials who were anti-Semitic. Some refused to cooperate unless bribed.

Throughout the 1930s conditions for the Jews in Germany worsened. Some people in the United States refused to buy German products in an effort to put pressure on Hitler, but it didn't help. The Jews who were unable to escape eventually ended up as victims of the Holocaust.

Hitler Conquers Europe

Hitler, of course, had other concerns besides the Jews. One of them was the enlargement of Germany's territory. Threatening to use force if he did not get his way, he gained control of Austria in 1938 and of Czechoslovakia in 1939. Later in 1939, when he invaded Poland, World War II broke out.

During the early years of the war, Hitler's armies conquered most of Europe. Millions of Jews were now under German rule, and Hitler felt he was at last in a position to solve the "Jewish Question." As Hitler saw it, the "Jewish Question" was simply the fact that Jews existed. The "final solution," therefore, emerged as a way to destroy them.

And this is what the Nazis and their supporters in many countries tried. Throughout Europe, in all the countries under their control—Poland, western Russia, Hungary, Czechoslovakia, Lithuania, Latvia, Bulgaria, Yugoslavia, Greece, Italy, France, Holland, Denmark, Norway—the Jews were rounded up and confined in concentration camps or ghettos. Stripped of their property, brutalized, terrified and disoriented, they were forced to work as slave laborers in abominable conditions. Many died of starvation and disease. Others were shot down or beaten to death.

As their war against the Jews progressed, however, the Nazis turned to large-scale centralized killing operations. Jews from all over Europe were loaded into trains and shipped to death camps—among them, Auschwitz, Treblinka, Sobibor.

The Death Camps

In the death camps, human life was destroyed quickly and "efficiently." Under the whips of cruel SS guards, the Jewish victims were herded off the trains and into gas chambers, where they were exterminated by poison gas within a few minutes.

All together, at least six million Jewish men, women, and children were killed by the Nazis, almost the entire Jewish population of the continent of Europe. Millions of

Adolf Hitler, Herman Goering, and Joseph Goebbels, the Nazi triumvirate.

non-Jews were also systematically killed—political opponents; Slavic peoples and other minorities—but in the case of the Jews the Nazis seemed determined to wipe an entire people off the face of the earth. They killed every Jew they could get their hands on, including infants, the elderly, and the sick.

Some Jews fought back against the Nazis at every possible opportunity. In work camps and factories, they sabotaged the German war effort. In the ghetto of Warsaw, the forests of Lithuania, and other places, they secretly gathered or made weapons and bravely attacked their Nazi tormentors.

Some Christians, too, tried to help. Taking great personal risks, they hid Jewish friends in their homes or cellars. Many of these righteous Christians were caught and killed by the Nazis. In the most famous instance of Christians helping Jews, the people of Denmark joined together to help the Danish Jews escape to safety in Sweden.

Two brave Jewish resistance fighters caught by the Nazis. They were executed on the spot.

A Jewish partisan.

But in most of Europe, people willing to take such risks were few and far between. And many Europeans, even if they hated the Nazis, also hated the Jews. They stood by and watched the work of destruction, and in many cases helped the Nazis to carry it out.

The Final Solution

To some Nazis the "final solution" was more important than anything else. Though Germany was hemmed in by enemies and fighting for its life, they diverted valuable resources to the extermination machine. Trains that could have carried ammunition to the front were used to transport Jews to the death camps. Soldiers who could have been defending their country were instead send to round up and guard Jewish civilians. After several years of war, Hitler knew he could not defeat America and the other Allies, but he was determined to win at least one victory by wiping out the Jews.

In 1945, Hitler committed suicide and Germany surrendered. The country was almost totally destroyed, but so too was European Jewry. The surviving Jews were weak, sick, starving, Known as "displaced persons" because they had no homes to return to, they were often scarred psychologically as well as physically.

Some of the displaced persons found new homes in the United States, Canada, Australia, South Africa and other countries. But as had been the case in the 1930s, immigration quotas were in effect, and only a limited number of survivors were welcome.

With most doors closed to them, the survivors looked to the ancient Jewish homeland—the land of Israel, then known as Palestine. Since World War I Palestine had been under British rule. Because the British wanted good relations with the Arabs, they

The UJA made a new life in the land of their forefathers possible for them. Here you see new arrivals, young and old, being helped as they disembark at Haifa.

THE PALESTINE POST

JERUSALEM
SUNDAY, MAY 16, 1948

PRICE: 25 MILS
VOL. XXIII. No. 6714

STATE OF ISRAEL IS BORN

The first independent Jewish State in 19 centuries was born in Tel Aviv as the British Mandate over Palestine came to an end at midnight on Friday, and it was immediately subjected to the test of fire. As "Medinat Yisrael" (State of Israel) was proclaimed, the battle for Jerusalem raged, with most of the city falling to the Jews. At the same time, President Truman announced that the United States would accord recognition to the new State. A few hours later, Palestine was invaded by Moslem armies from the south, east and north, and Tel Aviv was raided from the air. On Friday the United Nations Special Assembly adjourned after adopting a resolution to appoint a mediator but without taking any action on the Partition Resolution of November 29.

Yesterday the battle for the Jerusalem-Tel Aviv road was still under way, and two Arab villages were taken. In the north, Acre town was captured, and the Jewish Army consolidated its positions in Western Galilee.

Most Crowded Hours in Palestine's History

Between Thursday night and this morning Palestine went through what by all standards must be among the most crowded hours in its history.

For the Jewish population there was the anguish over the fate of the few hundred Haganah men and women in the Kfar Etzion bloc of settlements near Hebron. Their surrender to a fully equipped superior foreign force desperately in need of a victory was a foregone conclusion. What could not be known, with no communications since Thursday morning, was whether and to what extent the Red Cross and the Truce Consuls would secure civilized conditions for prisoners and wounded, and proper respect for the dead. Doubts on some of these anxious questions have now been resolved.

On Friday afternoon, from Tel Aviv, came the expected announcement of the Jewish State, and its official naming at birth. "Medinat Yisrael"—State of Israel, with the swearing in of the first Council of Government. The proclamation of the State was made at midnight, coinciding with the sailing from Haifa of Britain's last High Commissioner. Within the hour, President Truman announced in Washington that the Government of the United States had decided to give de facto recognition to the Jewish State, with Jer of Jewish settlements in North-Eastern Galilee.

The Security Council met yesterday in a special session to consider action on the invasion of Palestine by member states of the U.N.

In the afternoon, Jerusalem was subjected to shelling from the northwest.

Haganah forces throughout the country continued mopping up, and Jewish sources claimed most of Western Galilee safe against attack. Naharayim, near Jisr el Majamie, inside Trans-Jordan.

JEWS TAKE OVER SECURITY ZONES

The Battle for Jerusalem, which began when the British forces withdrew on Friday morning, continued all day Friday and yesterday. The crackle of small-arms fire and explosions of mortar shells were still being heard in the early hours of this morning as the battle entered its third day.

Repeated efforts on Friday evening and again on Saturday by the U.N. Truce Commission to bring about a "cease fire" were brought to nought when the Arab representatives failed to agree within the specified time limit.

On Friday morning, Jewish forces entered the Russian Compound and Zone C to occupy the buildings requisitioned from Jews last year. This operation was almost bloodless, but beyond the western edge of Zone C, Arabs engaged the Jews in Jaffa Road. The Arabs were forced back and the Barclays Bank area was taken.

In other parts of the city fighting flared up. Jews overran one after another the areas evacuated by the British. By last night, the quarters and

Egyptian Air Force Spitfires Bomb Tel Aviv; One Shot Down

Kol Israel, the Tel Aviv broadcasting station, reported noon that Tel Aviv had been bombed three times in the previous evening and morning, and that one plane had been shot down and its Egyptian pilot taken prisoner.

In the first raid, four planes attacked from a height of 300 feet. Two dropped bombs, while the others strafed the city. Little damage was caused. In the second attack two hours later, the airport to the north of the city was bombed, and an Air France plane parked there was damaged. The third raid was launched shortly before midday, but the planes were driven off without causing any damage.

Two settlements in the Negev had also been attacked from the air, the radio reported.

A country-wide blackout was ordered by Air Raid Precaution Headquarters in Tel Aviv.

Mr. David Ben Gurion, the Prime Minister, broadcast from Tel Aviv to the people of America yesterday morning. As he spoke, Egyptian planes were bombing the city.

In the north, the settlements of Ein Gev and Shaar Hagolan and Dan had been shelled, but no further details were available.

Kalandia airfield was taken by the Jewish army on Friday morning, shortly after the High Commissioner had left; there by plane for Haifa. The field was evacuated, together with the neighbouring settlement of Ataroth, on Friday night. The settlement itself was burnt by Arabs yesterday.

2 Columns Cross Southern Border
By WALTER COLLINS
U.P. Correspondent

CAIRO, Saturday. — A com-

Etzion Settlers Taken P.O.W.

Fighting in the Kfar Etzion bloc continued throughout Friday, after Kfar Etzion it-

U.S. RECOGNIZES JEWISH STATE

WASHINGTON, Saturday. —Ten minutes after the termination of the British Mandate on Friday, the White House released a formal statement by President Truman that the U.S. Government intended to recognize the Provisional Jewish Government as the de facto authority representing the Jewish State.

The U.S. is also considering lifting the arms embargo but it is not known whether to Palestine only or the entire Middle East, and the establishment of diplomatic relations with the Jewish Provisional Government.

The White House press secretary, Mr. Charles Ross, told correspondents today that reaction so far to the recognition had been overwhelmingly favourable. He said this step had been discussed with Mr. Marshall and Mr. Lovett before action was taken, and it had their complete support.

Mr. Ross said that the President had decided several days ago to grant American recogni-

Proclamation by Head Of Government

The creation of "Medinat Yisrael", the State of Israel, was proclaimed at midnight on Friday by Mr. David Ben Gurion, until then Chairman of the Jewish Agency Executive and now head of the State's Provisional Council of Government.

David Ben Gurion, Prime Minister

Special Assembly Adjourns

FLUSHING MEADOWS, Saturday. — The Special U.N. Assembly, called four weeks ago to discuss the U.S. propos-

The first act of the Council of Government, as announced by its head, was to abolish all legislation of the 1939 White Paper of the late Mandatory Power, particularly the Ordinance and Orders relating to immigration and land transfer.

In the declaration of independence, Mr. Ben Gurion called on the Arabs of Palestine to restore peace, assuring them full civic rights and full representation in all governmental organs of the State. Mr. Ben Gurion prefaced the declaration with a review of the historic connection of the Jewish people with the Land of Israel and of their efforts to return, which never ceased throughout the generations of their dispersal, until the Nazi holocaust proved anew the urgency of the need for a Jewish State.

The Balfour Declaration of 1917, confirmed by the League of Nations, had given explicit international recognition to the right of the Jewish

A banner headline announces the birth of a new state. Although the State of Israel was proclaimed on Friday afternoon, May 14, 1948, the paper is dated Sunday, May 16, because no papers in Israel are printed on the Jewish Sabbath.

21

refused to allow the Jewish survivors to settle there. Through Aliyah Bet, a secret illegal immigration set up by the Jewish resistance movement in Palestine, many displaced persons courageously ran the British blockade.

The State of Israel

In 1948, the State of Israel came into being. Now, at last, all Jewish survivors were welcome. Hundreds of thousands of displaced persons were now able to begin new lives under a Jewish flag.

Those who remember the Holocaust know that Jews were not its only victims. Once unleashed, the Nazi death machine was turned against other minorities and against all who spoke out for truth and

The refugee boat *Exodus 1947*. It was this boat that the British refused permission to enter Palestine.

freedom. When dictatorship holds sway, and intolerance runs wild, no one is safe in the end. Thus all people of good will, both non-Jewish and Jewish, are resolved that there must never be another Holocaust.

In America and many other countries, Jews live in peace and security. In other places, however, such as the Soviet Union and some parts of Latin America, Jews are still persecuted. In no part of the world has anti-Semitism totally disappeared.

The existence of the State of Israel is a guarantee that persecuted Jews will always have a safe haven. But persecution itself will not end until anti-Semitism and all other forms of religious and racial intolerance have been eradicated.

Israeli soldier praying at the Western Wall.

Nazis and the Holocaust

Something to Think About

In this section we learned how Hitler became active in politics and eventually dominated the government, turning it to his own ends. We learned how Hitler used the government to pass and enforce anti-Jewish laws. This raises the subject of government and what Judaism has said about it. Below are three passages from the Rabbis about government. Think about them and what each means.

Voices from Tradition

"Keep the king's command" (Ecclesiastes 8:2). The Holy Spirit says, "I beg you that if the earthly kingdom decree persecution, you shall not rebel in all that it decrees against you, but you shall keep the king's command. But if it decree that you should revoke the Torah, the Commandments, and the Sabbath, then listen not to the king's command. Thus did Hananiah, Mishael, and Azariah. But when deliverance came, they would not come forth (from the furnace) till the king commanded them."

— Tanhuma (Noah 19b–20a)

While discussing how the prophets foresaw what foreign empires would do to Israel, we find this negative expression about governments:

Rabbi Huna said: "All governments may be called by the name 'Asshur,' inasmuch as they made themselves strong (ashsher) at the expense of Israel." Rabbi Yosee ben Hanina said: "All governments may be called by the name Mitzrayim (Egypt), since they oppressed (metzerin) Israel."

The passage continues in much the same vein, using many different proof-texts and Hebrew puns to make the point.

— Leviticus Rabbah 13:5

"You make men as the fishes of the sea" (Habakkuk 1:14). As it is with the fishes of the sea, the one that is bigger swallows the other up, so with man; were it not for the fear of the government, every one that is greater than his fellow would swallow him up. This is what Rabbi Hanina, the prefect of the priesthood, said: "Pray for the welfare of the government, for were it not for the fear of the government, a man would swallow up his neighbor alive."

— Talmud (Avodah Zarah 4a)

And in Your Opinion...

Look at the first passage above again. Do you agree with the idea contained in it that a Jew should not rebel against a persecuting government unless it tries to annul the Torah, the Commandments, or the Shabbat? Why do you think the Rabbis would make such a statement? What do you know about the Rabbis that helps you understand the high priority this statement places on the Torah, Commandments, and Shabbat? Do you know about the Great Jewish Rebellion of the year 67 or about the Bar Kochba Rebellion? If you don't, ask your teacher to tell you about them in brief. Do you think the experience of the failed Great Jewish Rebellion and the failed Bar Kochba Rebellion influenced their thinking?

The second statement seems to say that governments always oppress Jews. Do you agree with that? Do you know enough about Jewish life under Roman rule to understand why the authors of this statement felt so negatively? A good project would be to write an article for your school newspaper about that early Jewish experience.

The third passage puts a great responsibility on the government. The government, at a minimum, is supposed to protect those under its authority from each other. But in Hitler's case we learned how he used the government itself to hurt people. It is as if a big fish used the government to help it swallow up other, weaker fish instead of the government protecting the weaker fish from the big fish. What do you think the role of government should be? Do you agree with the definition given in the third passage? Is there more to it than that? How can people see to it that government performs that role and isn't perverted into something else? These are very big and difficult questions. A good project would be to interview your parents, one of your teachers, or someone in authority at school or synagogue with these questions. How did they answer?

Klaus Heck

Innocence

I was born in the city of Dusseldorf on the Rhine in Germany. Our family was a middle-class German family consisting of my parents, a brother two years older than I, and myself. My father, after his return from fighting for four years in the First World War, obtained an excellent job working for one of the largest ironworks in Germany. The house in Cologne in which we lived was custom-built for us with adequate space to accommodate the family, a governess, a housekeeper, and a chauffeur. The chauffeur drove my father about in a large American car — a Buick.

My parents were both members of the Nazi Party, but it was my mother, not my father, who felt that Hitler was the right person to restore Germany to its greatest glory as it was prior to the war. My father was noncommittal about Hitler and rarely attended meetings. His main interest was in collecting great art, which he loved. In 1931 — when I was eight — my father, whom I loved dearly, died of a sudden heart attack, and from then on I always felt that something irreplaceable was missing in my life.

When I was ten years old, I joined a Christian youth movement similar to the YMCA and the Boy Scouts. Six months later this movement was dissolved by Hitler. Along with the country's other youth groups, it was replaced by a new organization — the "Hitler Jugend" (Hitler Youth). This group was designed to teach us that we were Germans, first and foremost, and that our chief duty was to support the Fuehrer with heart and soul.

In school we learned that Hitler would make our country the greatest in the world. As the weeks passed by, we noticed that a few of the older teachers were no longer there. They were replaced by younger teachers wearing emblems of the Nazi Party.

Adolf Hitler.

Our history teachers showed us how Germany, in comparison to other countries, was the role model for the world. For religious studies, the Catholic students were instructed by priests, and the Protestant students by history teachers. In both cases, however, the lesson was the same: after the older generation died off, German society would not require churches, since the Hitler Youth would know better. One of Hitler's slogans was, "Church-going is for the old." So to wean the youth away from the practice of attending church, the Hitler Jugend had activities on Sunday, such as marching and singing in the streets. Once we even hiked to Holland. Gradually, as I began to enjoy the "new religion" of Hitler, I forgot my love for Christmas and other Christian holidays.

One summer I was an exchange student in England, where I lived with an English family. The people I met in England asked how we Germans could tolerate a monster, a bandit, like Hitler as the leader of our government. If I had been able to speak English more fluently, I would have told them that thanks to our Fuehrer, we had no unemployment, beautiful new highways, and the average worker could now live in good housing and even take a vacation. "What's wrong with these people," I wondered. Didn't they know how the Austrians had welcomed us with open arms, screaming, "One people, one nation, one Fuehrer!" Even in our churches you could hear prayers for our leader Hitler because the people felt that he was the brightest star that heaven could have sent us.

In 1938, in Cologne, my friends and I attended a huge rally for our leader Hitler. We were filled with enthusiasm and admiration for our Fuehrer.

Hitler's Motto

"Hard as Krupp steel, tough as leather, swift as greyhounds," this was our motto in the Hitler Youth. It was good to feel superior,

A Jewish young man forced to paint the word "Jud" on the front of his house.

and our superiority came from following the goals of the Hitler Youth — respect for family, love of country, and obedience to officers and the government. The Nuremburg laws of 1935, which included prohibitions against mixed marriages, begging, idleness, and incurables, sounded reasonable to me because these people were a burden to our society. What a shock it was to hear that the incurables were gradually disappearing from the hospitals, that old generals were being replaced by younger men such as Rudolph Hess. I was certain that someone else, not Hitler, must be responsible.

When my brother, at the age of seventeen, criticized the editorials in German papers, he was warned by the police not to question the action of the government's paper. As I grew up, I became more involved in discussions concerning politics. During one of these discussions a friend told me that the Poles and Czechs were really not good people, that due to the Versailles Treaty we Germans had lost territories that truly belonged to us, and that Hitler wanted only

28

peace. "If it were not for those damn subhuman Jews, ruling the world and causing misunderstandings between people, there would be no danger of war," said my friend. I could not agree with him completely as I had a Jewish friend who did not seem to be like the Jews he described.

In 1938, a German official was killed by a Jew, and this brought on vicious mob attacks in Germany on the 9th and 10th of November. At this time in Germany there were about 69 million Germans and a half million Jews. The names of Dachau and Theresienstadt became familiar to all Germans because people accused of being traitors, spies, saboteurs, and communists were taken there. This did not disturb us. It seemed natural that those who did not obey the law should be locked up.

Life in the Army

At the age of eighteen, every German boy had to go into the army, and it was with a great deal of pride that we did so. Shortly after I became a soldier, I found myself on a

The Nazis burned Jewish books and books by Jewish authors. These storm-troopers are gathering carloads of books for destruction.

train — destination unknown. We eventually arrived in a small town in the Ukraine, where the people greeted us with flowers and cheers, and were very happy to see us. It was obvious that they preferred us to rule them instead of the Russians. That evening we were entertained by the actors

29

from the National Theater of Kiev. The following morning we were given bicycles and sent into the Russian hinterland. The roads were filled with young German soldiers, with heavy knapsacks on their backs, peddling their bicycles, singing German victory songs as they went along, apparently without a worry in the world. It was reassuring to know that our Fuehrer was in charge and all I had to do was obey orders.

After peddling 150 miles, tired and exhausted, we were met by the *Handsers,* regular army soldiers. It was then that we heard for the first time, from the *Handser* commander, that Germany had suffered its first air attack. At least the news from Africa was good, because Rommel, one of Hitler's generals, was pushing ahead against our enemies. It was hard to believe that enemy planes had been able to get past our superior Luftwaffe. It never entered my mind that we Germans were bombing countries and hurting people. I could only think of us as liberators, and believed that whatever we were doing was necessary in order to make the world a better place to live in.

Because of the rapid advance of the Russian army, we had to leave our positions on June 28, 1942. On the way we passed masses of Russian civilians moving slowly along each side of the road. Taking a closer look at these people, I noticed that they had long beards, black caftans, and wide-brimmed hats. With sticks in their hands, they were digging in the earth, and it soon became clear that they were being used as human mine-detectors. Standing at a safe distance, Hungarian soldiers were watching them. It was hard to believe that anyone could be so cruel, even to Jews. I wondered how such actions could be justified. My commander remarked that he would check into the matter when he called Berlin.

Weeks passed without any mail from home, and when news finally came, it was not good. Many cities in Germany were being bombed. We found it hard to imagine that only twenty-four years had passed since the First World War. Nevertheless, in this Second World War there was no doubt that victory would be ours and that all the fighting was worthwhile.

In a little town called Malinoska, just east of Moscow, one could enjoy looking at the lake and the whitewashed houses. I saw a stove in a house that was also used as a bed. I had never seen or heard of such a thing before. The townspeople seemed to be very contented people who managed to live simply without the worldly possessions that I was used to.

We were then moved by cattle cars, sleeping on straw-filled sacks and eating army rations. Though it was uncomfortable I did not mind giving a few of my precious young years to my country and my Fuehrer. When our train stopped to get more food, another train of cattle cars was blocking the path to the station. We were told to go under the cars to pick up our food. Once back in our own train we could smell the odor of a latrine. Then we realized that our uniforms were spotted with human excrement. Climbing out of the cars again, we looked around to see where it had come from. I realized it had fallen through the spaces between the planks that made up the floors of the cattle cars of the train next to us. On further examination of the trains, I found that all its windows were closed, but once or twice, through a crack, I could see a ghastly face staring at me. I told one of our officers about this, and, in annoyance, he warned me not to exaggerate what I had seen because it would cause embarrassment for Germany. It took only a few days to have my uniform cleaned, but it would not be as easy to cleanse our souls.

Regardless of what had happened, I still remained a loyal German soldier because I was deeply convinced that what we were doing was right. My anger centered on America for coming into the war to help the European countries. American interference, I felt, was delaying our victory.

During the winter of 1945, I was wounded in a battle in which most of my friends were killed. After fighting in Russia for two years and living through the freezing Russian winters, covered with ice and snow, I arrived at a hospital. On this very day Hitler spoke on the radio, reminding us of his great leadership during the past twelve years. His voice was deep and serious. Cold shivers ran up my spine as I listened to him and thought of how, during the past two years, he had been keeping us in the dark about certain things. We were told when we were 100 miles south of Moscow in June 1942, but never told how, in the winter of 1942–43, our forces were pushed back from Stalingrad by the Russian army, preventing our entering the city. Our Fuehrer, I felt, must have had a good reason for not giving us all the information about the war, and in my heart I knew that come what may, our Fuehrer was always right.

Escape

The Russian army continued to advance. As a wounded German officer, I knew I would be in serious danger if they caught me. Driven by the desire to stay alive, I found a way to get to the S.S. *Steuben*, formerly a ship of the Hamburg-America Line. Swarms of German soldiers crowded toward the ship. Since it could only hold 250 people, only a few of us could be rescued. It was up to the doctor to decide who was wounded severely enough to be allowed aboard. Many of those who were left behind drowned as they struggled to reach the ship.

My windowless cabin had two beds and one emergency cot. I was cleaned and washed, and my bandages were changed. At the hospital where I had been treated earlier, the doctors had been unable to remove the shell fragments imbedded in one of my wounds. Now, however, it was discovered that they had shifted position and worked their way out on their own. This was very lucky, for otherwise my wounds might have taken much longer to heal.

When I was served my first, long-awaited hot meal, my thoughts centered on family,

31

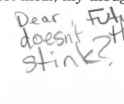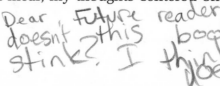

Dear Future reader, doesn't this book stink? I think it does

friends, and those who had not made it along with me. My thoughts were disrupted by a sudden jolt caused by a torpedo striking the ship. The first thing I did was to put on a life jacket even though the loud speaker announced that we were not in danger. Nevertheless, I soon found myself alone, floating in the Baltic Sea. In the darkness I could only see the illuminated face of my watch, which kept me awake and encouraged me to sing, one after another, the songs of my youth. Through the darkness came a ray of light searching the waters for survivors. I could hear voices, but no one heard or saw me. The ship passed, and suddenly I felt a feeling of hopelessness, but not for long. Once more the searchlights returned, with voices asking if anyone was there in the water. I screamed and yelled as loud as I could until a woman's voice called back, "There he is — there is someone in the water." I knew then that I would be saved, and then I could not remember anything because I had fainted.

A German mine-sweeper was my rescuer. But due to the lack of fuel it had to drop me and some other survivors off at a small town not yet taken by the Red Army. Not far away, in Kellberg, Germany, there was a German airfield with a hospital station. Once more, in an effort to save my own life, I lied to the doctor who was taking care of me, and instead of calling a girlfriend — as I had told him I was doing — I called the airfield. The officer in command told me I would have a better chance of getting home to Germany if I could somehow make my way to the airfield alone. He explained that he could not send anyone for me. After the phone call I asked the doctor for permission to go to see my girlfriend. He believed me and gave me a clean uniform to wear. Fortunately I saw a farmer with a horse and wagon on the road. He was kind enough to give me a ride to the airfield.

At the airfield, I heard on the radio that enemy troops were approaching Berlin and that Dresden was being bombed by the

American and English air forces. The report stated that many people had been killed. In the midst of all this, we Germans were being reminded of the danger of surrender and what would happen to us if we did. We were told that in the event of surrender the Jews would castrate every German man, rape our women, and starve us all. Over and over again this was drummed into our heads, and I believed it.

Going Home

Not long after my arrival at the airfield, I managed to get back to Germany and there ended up a prisoner of war. By March 18, 1945, we Germans knew that we had been defeated, and as far as I was concerned, it didn't matter. Since the P.O.W. camp was in France, I had only one fear: that we would be hit by a V-2 bomb, the new miracle weapon that we were sure would enable us to win the war.

In the camp we were questioned by an American lieutenant named Greenberg and examined to see whether we were members of the Waffen SS. This surprised me, as I had not known until then that SS men had special tattoos on their right arms. When asked about the death of the millions of Jews, none of us took it very seriously, and as a matter of fact, a few of us laughed.

Our only concern at that time was about what was happening to our country and our own lives. News of Hitler's death soon reached us in the camp, and even though we Germans wanted to honor and salute our leader, our American captors would not allow us to do so. In September 1945, with discharge papers in my hand, I made my way back to my home in Germany. There I found my mother, grandparents, and brother just back from Denmark. Germany had been defeated, but at least we were all still together, and soon we would be able to make plans for the future.

Dear future owner,
I hope you enjoy this Book and this class. Read this carefully.

abcdefghijklmnopqrstuvwxyz

The Last owner,
ReBecca Katcoff

Innocence

Something to Think About

Is the author of the story a war criminal? He describes himself as an ordinary soldier and says: "It never entered my mind that we Germans were bombing countries and hurting people. I could only think of us as liberators and whatever we were doing was necessary in order to make the world a better place to live in." But he also tells us he knew the Nazis were doing horrible things when he says: "When our train stopped to get more food, another train of cattle cars blocked the path to our station...we could smell the odor of a latrine. Then we realized that our uniforms were spotted with human excrement....I saw the wooden planks of the cattle cars of the train next to us....I saw that there were only closed windows, and once or twice I could see a ghastly face staring at me. I told one of our officers about this, and, in annoyance he told me not to exaggerate the things I saw because it would cause embarrassment for the Germans." Since it was clear to him that something ghastly was happening even worse than armies fighting each other, did he have a responsibility to do something about it?

Voices from Tradition

When God created the first man, God took him and let him pass before all the trees of the garden and said: "See My works, how fine and excellent they are. All that I have created has been given to you. Remember this and do not corrupt and desolate My world, for if you corrupt it, there is no one after you to set it right."

— Ecclesiastes Rabbah 7

Deuteronomy 20:2 teaches that before every battle, the "priest anointed for battle" had to read to the soldiers the rules and regulations on war, so that those rules could never be forgotten, never be taken for granted.

And in Your Opinion...

Above you were asked to think about whether this man was a war criminal or not. If you were the judge at this soldier's trial, and he defended himself by saying he never actually committed any war crimes, how would you rule? Is not actually committing the crime sufficient for innocence? Is knowing about the crime but not doing anything sufficient for guilt? Or is he both guilty and innocent?

Hanna Seckel

Hanna's Story

A Warm Kiss

When I was a young girl I lived in Prague, the capital of Czechoslovakia. I lived with my mother, my father, and my brother, Peter, who was four years younger than I. Education, religion, and the family circle were all very important to my family. I was very close to my aunts, uncles, and cousins; and on holidays we would all get together for large family gatherings. Although the family wasn't Orthodox and we didn't keep kashruth, we enjoyed the Jewish holidays and the family gatherings that accompanied them.

Unlike American children, I did not go to Hebrew school or Sunday school, because in our country religious education was provided in the public schools. For the Jewish children a rabbi would come in every day; for the Catholics, a priest; and for the Protestants, a minister. My school had children who belonged to all of these religions, and when I was a young girl I never had any problems getting along with children who weren't Jewish. Once in a while someone would tease me about being Jewish. I tried to think of something that I always kept in the back of my mind. I would think to myself, "If someone calls me a dirty Jew or some other word, I mustn't say anything about it, I mustn't make waves; I've got to learn to take it." This didn't happen very often and I soon became immune to remarks about my religion.

In the fifth grade I began going to a different school where I learned French. Soon I could speak three languages — French, German, and Czech. I enjoyed my new school very much and got along well with the other children and the teachers. I had a happy life with my family. My parents were very sports-minded, and they often took us children skiing or to soccer games. Every summer we rented a house in the country because our family really enjoyed the outdoors.

However, I had one big problem. Although I loved sports, none of the major sports organizations in Czechoslovakia would accept Jews for membership. When I was ten years old my parents let me join a Jewish organization called Maccabee.

Maccabee was part of the Zionist youth movement. The Jewish children who belonged participated in sporting events two or three times a week after school. I fit in very well with my new friends, and I soon felt as though I had always belonged with them.

Once I went on a five-week camping trip with my friends from Maccabee. We children lived together, learned Hebrew, and sang Jewish songs. We all became imbued with the pioneer spirit. Unfortunately my parents were not very supportive of my membership in Maccabee. They were very cautious about my involvement with Zionism. Despite the lack of support from my parents, I continued to belong to Maccabee.

I felt that I had found my niche in the world, and a group of friends with whom I felt comfortable. Even today my oldest friends are people I first met in Maccabee; like me, they survived the Holocaust, and many of them now live in Israel.

My father was a businessman, and we lived very comfortably in an apartment house in a neighborhood which was half Jewish. In 1938 an important event took place—the Nazis occupied a part of Czechoslovakia called the Sudetenland. My aunt and her family, who lived there, were forced to leave their home and move into our apartment. They warned my parents of how terrible the Nazis were, but my parents wouldn't listen. "What happened in Austria could never happen in Czechoslovakia," they said. "We are a democracy and we have a democratic President." Soon I began to notice a lot of new Jewish people in the neighborhood. They were refugees from Austria and Poland. They were running away from Hitler and the Nazis. Very often they left part of their family behind, and did not know what was happening back home.

The people in Prague were afraid that the Nazis would bomb Czechoslovakia. The government made everyone buy gas masks and carry them at all times. In school we had air raid drills instead of fire drills. Things grew worse and worse. In 1939, the thing that everyone had said couldn't happen, happened! The Nazis took over — our democratic government was destroyed, and Czechoslovakia became the German protectorate of Bohemia and Moravia.

Maccabee told all its members about what the Nazis were doing to the Jews in other countries. People even came from Palestine to awaken us. My parents were very angry about this. They said that the warnings were just propaganda to get children to go to Palestine. They said that the Zionist organization was exaggerating in order to get the young people to emigrate to Israel. Despite my parents' views, I definitely wanted to go to Palestine. All of us in Maccabee prepared ourselves in every way. We went to a training camp in the summer where we learned Hebrew and studied politics.

On day, in April of 1939, I went to

...gon Breslau • Schriftleitung, Vertriebsstelle u. Inseratenannahme: Gartenstraße 25, Fernsprecher 57277 • Postscheckkonto: Breslau 20136

Nummer 24   Breslau, den 27. Sivan 5695 / 28. Juni 1935   42. Jahrgang

Der Stand der Auswanderungsfrage

Von Dr. Arthur Prinz, Berlin

I.

Es war eine besondere Tragik für das deutsche Judentum, daß die nationalsozialistische Revolution gerade in eine Zeit fiel, in der die Auswanderungsmöglichkeiten im allgemeinen so gering waren, wie wohl niemals in den letzten hundert Jahren. Stand schon die ganze Nachkriegszeit in der überseeischen Welt im Zeichen wachsender Tendenzen zur gesetzlichen Beschränkung oder wenigstens Regelung der Einwanderung, so kam seit Ende 1929 als entscheidendes Moment hinzu, daß die großen überseeischen Einwanderungsländer — die Vereinigten Staaten, die britischen Dominions und Lateinamerika — durch den Zusammenbruch der Agrar- und Rohstoffpreise gleich zu Beginn der Weltwirtschaftskrise von ihrer vollen Schwere betroffen wurden und deshalb jede neue Einabzuwehren suchten. Dagegen konnten ...

suchen, die den Import an fremden Industrieprodukten verringern sollen. Nicht nur durch starken Zollschutz — der von den Regierungen oft schon gewährt wird, sobald in dem betreffenden Industriezweig auch nur Ansätze einer eigenen Erzeugung vorhanden sind! — sondern auch auf mannigfache andere Art wird die Errichtung neuer Unternehmungen unterstützt. Hier liegen zweifellos für denjenigen Teil unserer Auswanderer, die entweder als Unternehmer oder als einigermaßen ausgebildete Facharbeiter industrielle Kenntnisse besitzen, für die Zukunft verhältnismäßig große Chancen. Dies gilt auch für Handwerker und in gewissem Grade selbst für Kaufleute, besonders für Exportfachleute. Freilich ist nicht zu verkennen, daß die deutsche Devisenlage und -gesetzgebung für die Auswanderung von Unternehmern, da ja zur Errichtung neuer ...Hindernis bedeutet. ...

Aus dem Inhalt:

Unbelehrbare Agudas Jisroel
Arische Anwälte als Vertreter von Juden
Landlose Araber — Illegale Einwanderer
David Isak
Was geht in der Gemeinde Gleiwitz vor?

... ist die Lage fast verzweifelt. Viele Hunderte von ihnen sind, ...trung der Hicem, weiter gewand...

A German Jewish journal with an article on the possibility of emigration.

school and found the building occupied by German troops. The school was closed and the building was to be used as Nazi headquarters. A Nazi proclamation announced that it was now illegal for Jewish children to attend public school. Because of this restriction I became even more active in Maccabee and the Zionist movement.

As my brother grew older I became increasingly close to him. Peter was only ten years old, but he wrote poetry and songs and drew beautifully. He was brilliant and talented, and he even started a newspaper for Maccabee, after I got him involved in the organization.

I soon began to notice that parents were holding a lot of secret meetings in our house. I discovered they were planning to leave Czechoslovakia and go to Uganda, in Africa. Uganda was one of the very few countries in the world that would admit Jews at that time. Even the United States of America wouldn't permit any Jews who were fleeing the Nazis to enter the country. They had to wait for their quota. I worried about going to Uganda, and said the name to myself over and over again — Uganda, Uganda. I didn't want to leave my home and friends. But my parents never got the papers to emigrate, so our family was trapped under the Nazi regime in Czechoslovakia.

The Nazis made our lives miserable. Every day there were more rules for us to follow. One morning I went into the kitchen and found my mother sewing a bright yellow star with a black J onto my coat. She said, "Wear this with pride, as all of us will." This was 1939. Our ration cards were different from those of the rest of the population. Jewish store owners were forbidden to employ non-Jews. We also had a curfew. We Jewish children began to stay more to ourselves. We couldn't be with our Christian friends anymore, because they didn't want to play with us. Their parents wouldn't let them.

In the fall of 1939 I heard that the International League for Peace and Freedom was going to accept a certain amount of Jewish children between the ages of twelve and fifteen and take them to Denmark so that they could escape the Nazis. These children would live with Danish families and learn farming. I found out that I could go if my parents agreed to pay for the trip. In the winter of 1939 three trains, each carrying one hundred Jewish children, left Czechoslovakia for Denmark. Other trains left from Germany. I kissed my family goodbye in October of 1939. I wasn't too unhappy because I felt that I was setting out on some kind of fantastic adventure. Although we didn't know it, this was the last time I would see my family.

The Last Letter

The journey across Europe to Denmark was very happy for us. But our arrival in Denmark was very sad, especially when I had to leave my best friend, who had come with me on the train. I was taken to a farm in the Danish countryside. There was a family with four children, and they needed a maid. That became my job. But what a surprise to find no electricity or running water in the house. I never wrote this to my parents. I didn't want them to know. I wondered if my friends found the same conditions.

The farmer and his family were kind to me, but I had some very rough times during the winter. I worked very hard. I pumped water, cooked porridge, and did other difficult farm chores all day long. It was very cold that winter. I lived away from the house in a completely unheated room. It was so cold sometimes that when I woke up in the morning the blankets were frozen. I hadn't brought any boots from Czechoslovakia, so the farmer gave me wooden shoes which I stuffed with straw. Every morning I got out

of bed in the freezing room and went to the kitchen, where I chopped ice and heated it to make bath water. After kindling the fire I made breakfast for the entire family. Although life was hard I was not hungry, and I found ways to withstand the cold. Sometimes I heated a brick in the stove and took it to bed with me to keep me warm. My biggest problem was loneliness. All of my friends from Maccabee were scattered around Denmark. I did not know Danish so I couldn't communicate with the family at all.

I often received letters from my parents. These letters told of an increasingly worsening situation for the Jews in Czechoslovakia. Their jewelry and other valuables were taken, their ration cards were taken, and they were only allowed to go out on the street at certain hours. Five other families had moved into the same apartment with my parents. When these families moved out it was often because they were taken away by the Nazis in big vans. I found out later that they were all sent to concentration camps. I felt very lucky to be in Denmark.

In April of 1940 Denmark was occupied by the Nazis. One morning as I was doing my chores it seemed to me that the whole

German army came marching across the fields to the farm. All I could see were shiny black boots. I was terrified and didn't leave my room. After about a week on the farm the soldiers moved on.

In the spring of 1940, the farmer bought me a rusty bike and taught me how to ride it. I felt good. In the wintertime, because of the deep snow, I put ropes around the tires to make snow tires. In June of 1940 I moved to another farm near the town of Naestred which was where most of my Maccabee friends lived. Although I was happy to be with my friends again. I still had a lot of chores to do at my new home. I had to work in the fields, milk the cows, and feed the chickens. The worst job was emptying the chamberpots. My new unheated room was worse than the last one because it had a big crack in the wall where the cold air and wind blew in. But I was no longer lonely. A teacher came to teach us once a week. He taught us Zionism, Hebrew, and sometimes math.

Since the day when Jewish students were thrown out of schools, April 1–39, I haven't attended any classes. My parents always instilled in us the love for learning. Their saying was "What you know no one can take away from you." I was most eager to attend a school.

My Danish was quite good by now and I wrote to several boarding schools, asking to be accepted. I proposed to work for my tuition, to clean, to cook, to do anything which was necessary. Finally one school answered and took me up on my offer.

I was employed as a chambermaid for the headmistress of the local school. I cleaned the house and did other chores. I soon became very unhappy and lonely at the school. I wasn't paid for my work, so I could not afford to buy textbooks or uniforms like all the other girls had. I woke up early every morning and did the housework for the headmistress, and after that I attended classes at the school all day long. Every night after dinner I stayed up very late doing homework. I did not feel close to the other girls. I felt like Cinderella, everyone looked down at me. I realized that I was the only one who worked for her tuition. Their parents paid for the other students. I never told the other girls of my experiences, nor that I was Jewish, but they sensed that I was different. I did not live in the dorms with the others. I had to work most of the time, so I couldn't take part in the school activities or go to the dances. On the farm I had felt a part of the family, here I was an outsider. One morning I found that snow had come in through my window and washed away all the ink from the handwritten copies of my school work. All my notes were ruined. What was I going to do? How lucky that the school gave me a textbook as a Christmas gift. I accepted it, although deep down I knew that Christmas was not my holiday.

One of the saddest days in my life occurred in 1942 when I received a letter from my brother Peter saying, "I thought I would be Bar Mitzvah, but it doesn't look that way." He wrote, "That was the only thing I wanted to live for, my Bar Mitzvah." The tone of his letter worried me very much. Shortly afterwards a letter came from my parents. This one said simply, "This is the last letter. We have been selected." Tears filled my eyes as I read these words; I never heard from my family again. Later I learned they were sent to Auschwitz. The only survivors from my entire family were my uncle Pavel and I.

I began to learn a lot about anti-German feelings in Denmark. There was an organized resistance movement. German secrets were stolen and projects were sabotaged by the freedom-loving Danes. These people belonged to the underground. At the end of the year, I returned to Nespa and worked as a maid for a banker's family. It was not pleasant to be seventeeen years old and completely alone in the world. Still, I felt lucky to be alive. I didn't know about the gas chambers of Auschwitz, but I knew that my being here was better than being in Czechoslovakia.

It was now June of 1943. The Germans had occupied Denmark for over two years. They had not yet begun to persecute the Jews who lived here. Rumors were circulating that things would soon get worse. Danish Jews were leaving Denmark to go to Sweden, which was a neutral country. However, the Swedish government did not open their doors to the Jews. If Jews were caught trying to get into Sweden, they were sent to Germany to die in concentration camps.

Smelly Fish

In October of 1943 a young man from the Danish underground came to my house. He said that it was very dangerous for Jews to remain in Denmark. The Nazis were transporting Danish Jews to concentration camps in Germany. It was time for me to hide!

On a quiet, dark night he came to guide me to a secret place on the Danish coast. We found ourselves in a beautiful church which was a hideout for Jewish people and members of the underground who had to escape from Denmark. A week passed until a small fishing boat arrived to take us to Sweden. I had no money to pay for my passage. But I was allowed to get on the boat. It was a tiny boat that smelled of herring. We were covered up with straw, and a tarpaulin was placed on top, and over that were dumped hundreds of herrings.

Our trip to freedom had begun. The herring boat sailed. Ten hours later we were nowhere. It was Yom Kippur and we were worried. We knew the Germans always raided on Jewish holidays, and we didn't want

A photograph of the "Kattegat Bridge," a secret maritime link between Denmark and the British Isles. Arms for the resistance and Jewish refugees were transferred to Danish fishing vessels at sea.

to be trapped on the boat. We were surprised to find that the fisherman had no map and no idea of where he was going. After many hours at sea we landed in Poland. German soldiers with long bayonets rushed to inspect the boat and its cargo. My ears pounded as the soldiers with their guns walked around a few inches from our heads. We were afraid. Was this our last voyage? Did the fisherman know his way home?

We started out on the same long journey. Everyone was tired, seasick, and hungry. I discovered that one of the passengers on the boat was Rabbi Melchior, the Chief Rabbi of Denmark. The rabbi said to the fisherman, "I am the Chief Rabbi, and you have to take us to Sweden." The fisherman answered, "Rabbi, I put my life in danger to save all of you, and you know that if the Germans find you they'll kill me too. I want to reach Sweden as much as you."

Finally, after twenty-two hours at sea, we saw the Swedish coast in the distance. Dozens of people were rowing out to meet us, all yelling and waving hello. They came to take us ashore. What a great moment to at last reach the free and unoccupied ground of Sweden. Everyone laughed and cried on the beach; it was as if we had reached the promised land.

We were taken to a little fishing village near the coast. The Swedish people were so anxious to help that they argued about who would take us home for dinner. Rabbi Melchior and I went to a fisherman's house. There we found a delicious Swedish-style smorgasbord set out for us — sausages, cheeses, herring, dark bread and rye bread. What a wonderful sight for someone who hadn't eaten for four days. Later we were interviewed by a policeman. He took our fingerprints and photographs, and then we were taken to the local high school. For an entire week we lived in the high school gym because school was not in session. We left when the students returned. The other refugees went their own way. I was left alone, having no place to go I asked the officials of the school if they could find a job for me, and they offered me a job in their kitchen. I spent the next six months wearing a big burlap apron working in the kitchen of the school, cleaning herring with a fish knife. No luck in finding any of my friends, I had no idea if they were alive or dead. Working twelve hours a day without pay, I was happier than I had been in Denmark. I knew I was free.

It was fun to see street lamps and neon signs for the first time. As long as I could remember there had always been blackouts. I worked at the school until late in 1944. I was now eighteen years old and wanted to become a nurse. Attending a nursing school in northern Sweden, I made many new friends. We were taught to deliver babies and tend the sick. One of my first contacts was with a Czech Jewish family in Stockholm who made me feel as though I was one of them. From the radio we learned about the invasion of Normandy. My wish was that the war would end any minute so that I could find my family. I visited the Czech Embassy in exile, and found that my friends from Maccabee were safe in England, but they had no information about my parents and Peter.

Desperately in need of money, I left the nursing school and took a job in an insane sanitarium near University of Stockholm. Remaining there until 1945, I celebrated my twentieth birthday. In the summer of 1945 the Second World War ended; Hitler lost. First Germany and then Japan surrendered. I was working at the insane sanitarium when I heard the happy news. I was told that the Jews who has escaped from Denmark could go back and become citizens; so I eagerly returned to the country I had fled two years before. Arriving there, I found that this was not the case. I returned to Prague in 1946, but could find no information about my family. I wasn't even allowed to go back to my old home.

44

My uncle Pavel, my mother's youngest brother spent the war years in Russia. He returned to Czechoslovakia with the Red Army, as a liberator. He and I are the sole survivors of our big and loving family.

In 1948 I returned to Denmark because the Communists had taken over Czechoslovakia. I started feeling sorry for myself because of what had happened to me in the last ten years, and landed in the hospital. When I recovered, I got a job in Sweden as a translator. I applied to the American Embassy for permission to immigrate to America, but it wasn't until 1950 that permission was granted. Before I left Europe I took a trip to France and England. In 1950 I boarded the *Queen Elizabeth* for America and a new life. After surviving the Holocaust I know what freedom is.

I recorded this because the Cinderella story was a fairy tale. Mine was a true nightmare.

Hanna's Story

Something to Think About

Hannah speaks about her involvement with Zionism and her desire to go to Palestine. Hannah's desire was part of a very ancient Jewish value. Almost without interruption, since the Jews were exiled from the Land of Israel by the Romans, Jews have longed to return there. The ideal of aliyah (immigration to the Land of Israel) means participating in the rebuilding of a Jewish homeland by permanently living in the Land of Israel. Have you thought much about what aliyah means? Perhaps the passages below will be of help.

Voices from Tradition

Rabbi Meir used to say, "Anyone who dwells in the Land of Israel, the Land of Israel atones for him. As it is said, 'And no inhabitant will say, "I am sick"; the people who dwell there will be forgiven their sins' (Isaiah 33:24)." Still the matter is not well grounded. We do not know if their sins are cancelled by it or if their sins are held over in account by it. But it says, "And his land shall atone for his people" (Deuteronomy 32:43). Let it be their sins are cancelled by it and not held over in account by it. Therefore, Rabbi Meir used to say, "Anyone who lives in the Land of Israel, says the Shema morning and evening, and speaks the holy language, behold, he is a member of the world-to-come."

— Sifre Deuteronomy (Piska 333)

"And spirit to them that work therein" (Isaiah 42:5), said Rabbi Jeremiah ben Abba, in the name of Rabbi Johanan, (teaches) that whoever walks four cubits in the Land of Israel is assured a place in the world-to-come.

— Babylonian Talmud (Ketubot 111a)

And in Your Opinion...

1. We learned a lot about what happened to Hannah in Europe. What do you suppose her life would have been like if she had gone to Palestine? Do you know enough about what the Jewish community in Palestine was like at that time to form an opinion? Look up "Yishuv" in a Jewish encyclopedia and see.

2. Hannah tells us that her parents were not happy about her participation in a Zionist youth group. Do you think they were afraid that they would never see her again if she went to the Land of Israel? But the rabbinic passages above tell us how important living in the Land of Israel has been in the Jewish heritage. What do you think you would have done if you were Hannah? Before you answer, be sure to think about reasons why she should have gone to Israel and reasons why she shouldn't have gone.

David in the Mining Town

I was born in Dabrowa Gornicza, a little mining town in Poland, 17 kilometers from the German border. Besides my mother and father, I had a brother and a sister. My mother had seven brothers and sisters, and so did my father. Our entire family, including aunts, uncles, and cousins, lived in our little town. I could hardly pass a street without meeting one of my relatives. It felt good having such a large family and being able to celebrate our Jewish holidays together.

In our town, Jews were not permitted to work in the mines and steel mills. Most of the Jewish population owned or worked in small businesses of various kinds — shoemakers, butchers, grocers, and so forth. My father was a tailor with his own shop, and several other Jewish tailors worked for him.

The school I attended had very few Jews. This was not unusual, as the Jewish population in our town was very small. At the age of seven, I started public school, learning reading, writing, Polish history, and languages. On weekdays we also went to Hebrew school (cheder). The public school had classes six days a week, but my Jewish friends and I did not attend on Saturdays, because every Saturday morning we were at services in the synagogue. My Christian "friends" would give me the assignment that I missed in Saturday's class only after I gave them some cake or challah. Sometimes I would have to buy their "friendship" with my last penny. I grew up with a strong feeling about what it meant to be a Jew. From as early as I could remember, I frequently heard anti-Jewish remarks. Particularly on Sundays, if I was near a church, the children would come out filled with hatred against the Jews and eager to beat and degrade us. I learned at an early age that all the money in the world cannot buy friendship and erase the hatred against the Jews.

After seven years I went on to a private commercial school in the neighboring town of Bendzin. The teachers here were Jewish, and indeed, so was almost the entire population of the town. On the streets I often saw the Orthodox Jews, their heads covered, wearing black coats and twisted belts. Many of them were bearded, with payot, which reminded me of the Jews in our town. Orthodox Judaism, at that time, was the only type of Judaism practiced. Conservative and Reform Judaism were unheard of. My father and some of his friends did not dress like the very Orthodox Jews, but followed all the Jewish laws as required.

Our home was a modern Jewish home where my friends could come and listen to the gramophone (record player) and boys and girls could dance together. This togetherness made me feel good as a Jew, but it also made me unwilling to join the Boy Scouts or any other non-Jewish organization. My father, who believed strongly in a Jewish homeland, encouraged my friends and me to start our own Jewish youth group. We set up a local chapter of Gordonia. This organization was named in honor of A.D. Gordon, a famous Zionist leader. It was an enjoyable time of my life. We wore uniforms that looked like the ones worn by the Scouts, and we learned Hebrew songs and dances.

In 1937, pressure against the Jews increased. The Polish government prohibited kosher meat slaughtering. Visitors to our house from Germany told my father about the anti-Semitism there. This information came as a surprise to him because he had spent ten years of his young life in Germany. He remembered the Germans as polite and educated people who would not do anything wrong. So he called what he heard false propaganda.

In September 1939, the Germans invaded Poland. The Polish people of our town said they would never surrender, but when the Germans came, there was no resistance.

During the first few weeks of the German occupation the German police, in their green uniforms, treated both Jews and non-Jews the same. So the Jews in town believed that what they had heard about German anti-Semitism was false. As soon as the Gestapo, the German secret police, was put in charge of our town, everything changed. They were a group of young men between the ages of twenty and twenty-five, dressed in black uniforms. They went from street to street, marking Jewish stores, confiscating anything they desired. We Jews had to obey their orders because no one was willing to help us. If I didn't wear my armband with its Magen David on it, I was reported to the SS by my Polish "friends." We were not allowed to go to school, the library, or the movies, and we had to clean the streets and shovel the snow.

Late in 1939, the Germans assigned some of the Jewish men and older boys to forced labor. When I registered to take my father's place, they promised to pay me for my work, but they never did. I worked during the day for the Germans and returned home each night. One night, when I came home, my frightened mother greeted me with a notice to appear at the SS office. I didn't go, and one of my father's Christian friends hid me. After twenty-four hours of hiding, my father came to bring me some bad news. The

Ghetto work card of Chaim Joseph Orner, age 13.

SS had taken my mother as a hostage in my place. I decided to free my mother and went home to pick up a a few personal items before reporting to the SS headquarters. Not knowing that this was the last time I would ever see my father, I embraced him, saying goodbye. He placed his hands on top of my head and blessed me. The sight of my mother being released filled me with mixed emotions.

Camps and More Camps

I arrived at Blechame Camp in Germany in May 1942. There, my job was to assemble parts for barracks. The supervisors were German labor commanders. They were older than the German soldiers and wore different uniforms. We worked in a region where electricity was generated by coal. The engineers were Polish professionals. Also, there were Hungarian, French, and Belgian prisoners taken after Germany occupied their countries. In December 1942, trains brought coal to us from many different parts of Europe. I survived working there six days a week from early in the morning until late at night, living only on watery soup and a quarter of a loaf of bread a day, and the only place I could call home was the barracks.

The barracks was sparsely furnished, with bunk beds lining the walls and a long table in the middle, with benches on either side. Most of the time I lay on my narrow, hard bed; the space allotted me was so small that I couldn't sit up without hitting my head on the bunk above. To walk around was even harder because there was little space. Since the Germans hadn't yet taken away our belongings, I wore whatever clothing I had. To identify us easily, the Germans removed some cloth from our shirts and in its place inserted a yellow star on which was written *Jude* ("Jew").

We were separated from the non-Jews and told not to talk to them. However, whenever there was an opportunity, we secretly paid them with whatever belongings we had to bring us packages and letters from home. The camp was not far from our homes, and the non-Jews were permitted to come and go each day.

A Dutch Jewish badge with the inscription "Jew and non-Jew stand united in their struggle," distributed by the Dutch underground, 1942.

A truckload of Jewish prisoners being transported to their final destination.

After completing the work that the Germans wanted us to do, we were loaded into a boxcar and moved to another camp.

During the journey, I noticed that there were other passengers besides the ninety-five young Jewish boys, ages sixteen to seventeen in my group. We had been selected from the first camp to be part of a transport made up of Jews from Belgium, Holland, and Czechoslovakia. These people were professionals who had been in many camps. Talkig with them, I coud sense their confusion about being taken so far from their homes. Some of those from the East stayed in the East, and those from the West were taken to the East — a method invented by Hitler to separate families in such a way that they should never meet again. Throughout the journey I was filled with fear and kept looking at all the faces in the hope of finding someone from my large family.

Finally, we arrived at Gross-Rosen, another camp in Germany. This time our sleeping quarters were in a four-story building. It was clean, and there were sheets and blankets. There was food, just enough so that I did not feel hunger, but I never saw or tasted eggs, butter, milk, juice, or any kind of sweets. I was able to work six days a week and managed to stay well. Our job was to build another camp, which we did.

My Sister

Soon I was relocated to another camp. It looked like a small town and had two thousand inmates. These people were different. They were soldiers from Belgium, Russia, and Holland who had been captured fighting for their country. Their families were at home, and they were allowed to write to them. At first I did not know that there were 160 Jewish women working in the camp. Their jobs were to cook, clean, and sew for the Germans.

One day, as I was walking to work, I saw a group of women. In the middle of the group there was a familiar face. It must be an illusion, I thought. She is so much like my sister. The woman's hand raised in a wave, but quickly went to cover her mouth, reminding me to keep silent. I was filled with excitement, wanting to reach out for her, to hug her, but I could not. There was danger everywhere. This was the longest day of my life. I waited for the opportunity to be near her, to ask about the family and just to be able to touch her hand.

Somehow we managed to seek each other in the evening. We both wanted to speak openly about the family, but we didn't. Our conversation was mainly about what was happening in the camp and to us personally. My sister's job was to supervise the women, and mine was to make briquets for use in generating electricity. We were kept alive as long as we could work for the German war machine.

I was glad that my sister was never around to see it when the SS guards beat me. They didn't need any particular reason to inflict pain upon us. If my head turned slightly or I did not stand straight enough, they would beat me with their rifle butts. Sometimes they used clubs or other things to beat us.

Early in January 1944, I was taken to Mauthausen, a forced-labor camp that later became a concentration camp, and I never had a chance to say goodbye to my sister. I wondered if we would ever be together again; my world became so empty. Nothing mattered anymore. In this camp they tattooed me. My number was *104027*. The plan was set. Our identities were lost. My number was now my only name, and supposedly my death sentence as well. The Jews were being counted and branded like cattle, starting with the number one in Auschwitz and continuing throughout all the concentration camps in Europe.

Survival

Mauthausen did not have gas chambers which could kill many people at once, but was equipped with a crematorium to burn dead bodies. We could not escape death because it always surrounded us. Jews who gave up hope would touch the electrified barbed wire that encircled the camp, and others took their own lives by hanging. When the SS wanted some "fun," they

would come into our barracks and shoot at random. Each time I would hold my breath, thinking it might be my last, as the bullets flew around the room. When the German guards ran out of bullets or the desire to kill passed, I thanked God, with the *Shema* on my lips, for letting me remain alive.

It was a bitter cold day in January 1945, 20 degrees below freezing, when we were evacuated from the camp. We wore only the striped, thin uniforms, and most of us had wooden clogs on our feet, without socks. I had stuffed paper under my uniform to keep warm and unlike the others was wearing shoes, I was lucky because I had youth on my side. My will to live was strong, and I did not want to die. The walking never seemed to end. As I pushed myself to keep up the pace, I saw others around me falling (as they slid out of their wooden clogs). Some were unable to get up again. After two weeks of walking we arrived at a railroad station. Before us stood open boxcars which we entered with difficulty, barely able to lift our feet. Our journey continued for two more days, ending at a camp called Buchenwald. Of the original four thousand, only fifteen hundred of us were left. We stood there more dead than alive.

Before us we saw a long wall made of concrete blocks with a gate in the middle. On top of the gates were the German words *Arbeit Macht Frei*, meaning "Work makes you free"! As we walked into the camp, a sea of faces with bulging eyes in deep-set sockets appeared before us, their gaunt expressions clear proof that this was no work camp and its inmates were not free!

The SS men, shouting, ordered us to go to a certain area where we took showers and were disinfected. I was given a clean uniform, and as I put it on, I wondered whether it had been taken from a dead Jew.

Going to my assigned quarters, I noticed piles of dead bodies outside of each building, but I did not want to look, for fear I would recognize someone there. I couldn't even think about my parents, sister, or brother. I was incapable of doing anything except following orders.

The barracks were small and crowded, and the smell was terrible. The beds were narrow like in Blechame. Despite the smell, it was better to stay inside than to go out in the freezing cold. At least inside we were a little warm. With each day the pile of dead outside the barracks grew higher, and the familiar faces inside disappeared. During my stay I met an uncle who had survived Auschwitz. We did not embrace or kiss. Our bodies could not express any joy, nor could we speak of future hope. I did not see him again because we were shipped out to an unknown place, 120 of us jammed into a small overcrowded boxcar. In my pocket were my only possessions — one matchbox filled with sugar, and another filled with salt. As I watched one person after another die in the darkness beside me, I decided to share my precious belongings with another Jew. I forgot my selfishness for fear that I would be left alone. This man became my best friend. Of the 120 who began the journey, the seven of us who survived could not walk. Our bodies were filled with terrible pain. Even crawling out of the boxcar when it stopped was difficult, but we managed to get to a nearby stream, where we ate the soggy leaves floating on it. We also stole some sugar from another boxcar near us.

We were not told the name of the new camp, nor did we care. We had lost our identities, being called neither by name nor by number. Our guards were well-dressed, well-fed young men, wearing yellow shirts and brown pants, with swastikas on their arms. They belonged to the Hitler Youth and had been trained to beat every Jew who crossed their paths. I thought I had been through hell before, but this was even more terrifying. The Hitler Youth were worse than wild animals. I wished for death, but instead I was taken to work in a factory where we made antitank grenades. My job was to fill them with powder. We knew they would be used against the Americans and Russians, but we had no choice except to do as we were told. We also knew that we would eventually turn yellow and die from inhaling the powder, and as I watched it happen to several of my fellow Jews, I wondered whether I would be next.

Gradually the faces that guarded us changed. The SS and the Hitler Youth disappeared, and people from the surrounding towns were left to watch us. It was then that I learned the name of the camp, Flossenburg. Something told me that our liberation was near. My friend and I went into the kitchen and found some coffee grounds on the floor. Falling on the floor, we ate them.

The American Red Cross were the first to find me as I lay near the crematorium. They put me in a car and took me to a field hospital. I was unconscious and do not know how long I was in the hospital. Being unconscious helped me to survive, because unlike other prisoners, I was unable to overeat, a practice which cost many of them their lives. The German townspeople were ordered by the Americans to take care of the sick in the hospital. They washed and fed us.

This is the first time in forty years that I have been able, with difficulty, to tell my story. I have done so because I know that those who wanted to destroy the Jewish people deny that all this happened and perhaps are disappointed that their "final solution" did not work.

David in the Mining Town

Something to Think About

In this story, David turned himself over to the SS because they had taken his mother. He traded himself for her. Once taken he never saw his father again. His behavior informs us how important David's parents were to him. Honoring parents is an age-old Jewish value. Have you ever carefully thought about the meaning of honoring your parents? The events of this story provide you with an opportunity to think about this most basic of Jewish values. Perhaps the following material from the Babylonian Talmud will help you.

Voices from Tradition

The Rabbis say: Three combine (in the making of) human beings: God and father and mother. If people honor their father and mother, God says, "I reckon it to them as if I dwelt among them, and as if they honored Me."

Whenever Rabbi Tarfon's mother wanted to get up on to her bed, he bent down, and she would step upon him. When he came to the house of study and boasted of it, they said, "You have not fulfilled half of the commandment to 'honor.' Has she thrown your purse into the sea before you eyes, and you did not put her to shame?" When Rabbi Joseph heard the footsteps of his mother, he said, "I rise up before the Shechinah (God's nearness) which is approaching."

In what does reverence for a father consist? In not sitting in his presence, and in not speaking in his presence, and in not contradicting him. Of what does honor for parents consist? In providing them with food and drink, in clothing them, in giving them shoes for their feet, in helping them to enter or leave the house. Rabbi Eliezer said: "Even if his father order him to throw a purse of gold into the sea, he should obey him."

— Talmud (Kiddushin 30b–31b)

And in Your Opinion...

Having read the story and thought about the selections from the Talmud, did David do the right thing in trading himself for his mother? Is that what you would have done if it had been you? Try making two lists. On one, list the reasons you can think of that support his decision. On the other, list the reasons against his decision. Which list is more persuasive?

Arie Shnaper

Young Dreams

Young Dreams

I was born in Vilna, the largest Jewish community in Poland. Approximately 60,000 Jews lived there. Many of them lived in an exclusively Jewish neighborhood. On my street, however, there were both Jews and non-Jews. I was always very proud that Vilna was my birthplace because many famous Jews had their roots there. For instance, Rabbi Hillel, the author of *Beth Hillel*, and Rabbi Shabbetai ben Meir ha-Kohen, also known by the acronym "Shach," as well as Rabbi Elijah, the Vilna Gaon (1720-1797), who was considered the greatest rabbinical luminary, just to mention a few.

My father died when I was three months old. My mother never remarried. I never had any sisters or brothers. My mother earned a living as a dressmaker. We lived with my mother's sister and her family.

I attended a Jewish day school that was part of the Tarbuth Schools. The name of my school was "Beth Sefer Amoni" (The People's School). In addition to studying mathematics, science, and all other required secular subjects, I was taught Jewish history, Yiddish, and Bible. My formal education ended when I was fourteen because I had to go to work. A bookbinder took me on as an apprentice, and this became my lifelong profession.

I belonged to a Zionist youth organization called Hashomer Hatzair, where I had many good friends. Together, we enjoyed hiking, swimming, and scouting. However, our main goal was that one day we would all go to Palestine and rebuild the land of the Bible. After my friends graduated from college we went to a training farm to prepare ourselves for making aliyah. I learned to operate tractors and other farm machinery, ride horses, milk cows, and raise chickens. But best of all, I liked to grow vegetables and became an expert at growing tomatoes, which I still enjoy doing. The farm was able to accommodate 150 young Zionists. We were a large and happy family.

A Different Vilna

On September 1, 1939, Germany invaded Poland. This was the beginning of the Second World War. All of us had to leave the farm. It took me ten days to get back to Vilna, but I made it home. It felt good to see my family, sleep in my own bedroom, and eat my mother's cooking. Walking in the streets of the city and looking for my friends, I was shocked to find so many unfamiliar faces. I

A family on the way to the Ghetto.

59

was told that they were Jews from the surrounding villages who had left their homes and flocked to Vilna. Within a few weeks the Jewish population rose to 80,000. Meanwhile, the Germans quickly defeated the Polish army, Germany took the western part of the country, and the Russians took over the eastern part. A week after I arrived home, the Russians turned Vilna over to Lithuania. It was then that I saw my first pogrom. Lithuanian soldiers burst into Jewish homes, destroying whatever they didn't want, and looting valuable and precious objects. Household articles were thrown into the streets, torn bed pillows were tossed through windows; the falling feathers reminded me of a snowstorm in the middle of summer. In 1940, after the Soviet Union annexed Lithuania, Russian tanks rolled into Vilna. Many Jews lost their businesses and were forced to look for work, but there just wasn't any work for them. My mother lost most of her clients and I wondered how we would survive. Little did we know that what we lost under the rule of the Lithuanians and Russians would be nothing compared to our life under German rule.

On June 24, 1941, the Nazis launched a surprise attack. They destroyed the Russian airfields and all of the Russian planes. I heard many bombs falling and saw the railroad on fire. The flames brought back memories of sitting around a peaceful campfire with my friends, singing songs and listening to ghost stories. The German attack came so suddenly that the Russians were caught unprepared and the city fell into German hands without any resistance. Of all the different military uniforms that I saw, the black uniforms of the SS frightened me the most.

Each day, the Germans issued new restrictions against the Jews. We had to wear a yellow star sewn prominently onto our outer clothing, to make sure that we would be identified as Jews. We were not allowed to walk on the sidewalks — they were for human beings, according to the invaders, not for Jews. Everyone had to wait in line for food, but when milk and bread became scarce, Jews were forced to go to the back of the line and then, after hours of waiting, were told, "no more." The Gestapo raided Jewish homes in the middle of the night and

took fathers and sons away, supposedly for work gangs. Many of them never returned. Every night, when I went to sleep, I wondered whether it would be my last night in my own bed. Even in my own home I didn't feel safe.

The people rounded up in the Gestapo raids were taken to a place called Ponar, 10 kilometers from Vilna, where the SS killed them and piled their bodies into huge trenches. With this in mind, I decided I would try not to fall into the hands of the Nazis. I spent sleepness nights listening for the sound of Nazi boots or trucks coming, perhaps to take me away. When I heard them approaching my house at night, I jumped out of my bedroom window and hid near a lake not far from my home. One night my luck ran out. Breathless, I arrived at my secret hiding place. Two SS men were there, waiting for me, with guns in their hands. They ordered me to follow them, taking me in a truck to the city jail, where hundreds of Vilna Jews were being held. I spent three days in jail, hungry, thirsty, and frightened. The name "Ponar" was whispered over and over again. No one wanted to believe that whoever was taken to Ponar never returned. I remembered Ponar as a beautiful town where my friends and I had camped in the summertime, singing Hebrew and Yiddish songs around the fire, and dreaming of Palestine. In the winter I used to go sledding and would watch some of my friends skiing down the large and small hills. While sitting on the floor in jail, dreaming about being free, I was saved by my cousin, who brought my German identity papers to Gestapo headquarters. The papers proved that I had been working for the Germans. On my way home I was very nervous, looking back constantly, wondering if I would hear SS boots running after me or feel their hands on my shoulders.

The white *shaynen*, the work permit for the Jewish forced laborer in the service of the German army.

Through the Gate

Early one morning, not yet ready to get out of bed, I was awakened by the sound of screams, whistles, and yells. I jumped out of bed and looked out the window. German police and SS men were blowing their whistles to make sure that everyone heard their orders. Within fifteen minutes, they shouted, we all had to leave our homes, ready or not. I couldn't decide what to take, but my mother advised me to gather as many of my possessions as I could carry, and especially anything of value. As I walked with my mother, looking in all directions, the streets were black with people, some being pushed by SS men with bayonets. It was a hot day. Children were crying and parents tried to keep families together. There were old men holding their life's belongings in one hand and their *taleisim* (prayer shawls) in the other. All told, from various parts of the city 40,000 Jews were assembled and driven into the Ghetto.

When I passed through the wooden gates of the Ghetto, I breathed a sigh of relief, for we were no longer being herded through the streets by Lithuanians and Germans. I thought I had left my oppressors outside; how could I know that there was only an entrance to the Ghetto — no exit! Although 40,000 Jews had already perished, there were still too many of us for one Ghetto, so the Germans created a second, known as the smaller Ghetto. That was where my mother and I ended up.

As we entered, we were directed to a house that would have been occupied by a family of four or six people under normal conditions; now twenty-five or thirty of us were crammed in. Everybody was searching for a place to sit or sleep. I was lucky. My mother found an empty space under a table and that became my bed. In the Ghetto there were Jewish police called "Kapos." At first they joined because it was a secure job. They had good clothing (uniforms), better rations, and a comfortable place to live. Their work was not as hard as the forced labor I had to do, and they never suffered the humiliation of being beaten and embarrassed at work. They took orders from the SS. When the Germans needed five hundred or a thousand people, the Kapos went from house to house and rounded up the required number. I could never have done that to another human being. My friends and I were asked to join the police force. We were promised that if we followed orders, we would be among the only ones to survive the war. No Germans would ever harm us! We would be safe! I knew, however, that the Germans could not be trusted, and I was right. When the SS began liquidating the Ghetto and sending transports to the concentration camps, the Kappos could not hide, they were told to "follow the other Jews."

In the Ghetto there was a very active Jewish theater. Several of my friends were in a play called *Der Abiger Yid,* "The Indestructible Jew." Going to synagogue, praying, and studying about our religion were absolutely forbidden. The Germans wanted to break

A squad of Jewish police (Kapos) at a Dutch camp where batches of prisoners were assembled for the extermination camps. After they performed their murderous service they too ended up in gas chambers and mass graves.

the Jewish spirit and morale. Many people lost their will to live, but I was too stubborn to give in. After surviving a long, hard day of forced labor, with very little to eat, I dragged my exhausted body to the library. I was determined to keep my mind alive. It was the only thing they couldn't take away from me.

One Yom Kippur evening, as the Germans returned me to the Ghetto, I felt both happy and scared, having hidden a few small potatoes in my pockets. I was afraid of being caught at the gates. Once inside, a strange quietness surrounded me. The Ghetto was empty. They had taken my mother. I was alone and had no one with whom to share my potatoes.

Searching for a hiding place, I went up to the roof of the house. I lay down in the gutter, which was big enough for me, as I had lost so much weight. Contemplating my next move while looking over the quiet, empty streets, I saw my cousin and an SS guard in the distance. I wondered why they were walking together. When they came closer I realized that they were talking quietly, and I decided to reveal myself. This SS man was different. He had come to save Jews, not to kill them. With his help, the few remaining Jews were smuggled into the large Ghetto. When this German put his life in danger to save a few Jews, it gave me hope. I knew that even if there was only one in a million who cared about human life, I still had a chance to survive.

Young Dreams

Something to Think About

Near the end of this story we read that the "German goal was to break the Jewish spirit and morale," by forbidding Jewish praying and studying. Yet the author tells us he would go exhausted to the library to keep his mind alive. This story is reminding us of a very important Jewish value—the importance of Jewish study. How important do you think Jewish study is? Perhaps the following passages from rabbinic tradition will be of help.

Voices from Tradition

Once Rabbi Tarfon and the elders sat in the upper chamber of the house of Nitzah in Lydda, and the question was raised, "Is study greater or doing?" Rabbi Tarfon said, "Doing is greater." Akiba said, "Study is greater." Then they all said that study is greater, for it leads to doing.

— Talmud (Kiddushin 40b)

Rabbi Akiba was the shepherd of Ben Kalba Sabua'. When his daughter saw how pious and capable Akiba was, she said to him, "If I became engaged to you, would you go to the house of study?" He said, "Yes." So she became secretly betrothed to him, and sent him off. When her father heard of it, he expelled her from his house, and vowed that she should inherit none of his property. Akiba went and stayed twelve years in the house of study, and when he returned, he brought twelve thousand disciples with him. He heard an old man say to his (Akiba's) wife, "How long yet will you live a life of living widowhood?" She replied, "If he listened to me, he would stay away another twelve years." Then he thought, "It would happen with her permission." So he returned and stayed in the house of study another twelve years, and when he came back he brought twenty-four thousand disciples with him.

When his wife heard of his coming, she went out to meet him. Her neighbors said, "The righteous man knows the soul of his beast" (Proverbs 12:10). When she came to him, she fell down and kissed his feet. His disciples began to push her away; but he said, "Let her be; what is mine and what is yours is hers." When her father heard that a learned man had come to the city, he said "I will go to him; perhaps he will cancel my vow?" He said, "If he (Akiba) had known only one section or one halakah, I should not have made the vow." Then Akiba told him who he was. Then he fell down and kissed Akiba's feet, and gave him half his possessions.

— Talmud (Ketubot 62b)

64

Abbaye said: "We have received the teaching that 'poor is he who is poor in knowledge.'" In the west they say, "He who has knowledge has all; who has no knowledge, what has he? He who has got knowledge, what does he lack? Who has no knowledge, what has he?"

— Talmud (Nedarim 41a)

And in Your Opinion...

Do you think study is really that important? Is knowledge really everything, the way the above rabbinic passages say? Does Jewish study really keep the Jewish spirit alive? How much Jewish study do you do? How does it make you feel? You can try to answer these questions by making two lists. The first would be a list of reasons why Jewish study doesn't keep the Jewish spirit alive. The second would list reasons why Jewish study does keep the Jewish spirit alive. After reading over your lists, which is more convincing?

Errikos Sevillias

Darkness in the Synagogue

I was born in Thessaloniki, a large city in the north of Greece, and lived in Athens, the capital of Greece, with my family. My brother was killed fighting for our country against the Turks. When I grew up, I owned a leather goods store, and I lived a happy life with my wife and young daughter until disaster came at the beginning of World War II.

Early in 1941, Greece was occupied by the German and Italian armies. I became especially afraid and worried for my family because we were not only Greek citizens but also Jews. I knew about the Nazi anti-Semitism, but I really did not understand it, because there had been little anti-Semitism in Greece. In the beginning everybody suffered under the iron fist of the Nazis; since the Jews were not singled out for any special punishment, we believed that we would not be harmed.

In the spring of 1943, the chill of winter was still in my store, yet I could feel the air outside gradually getting warmer. The trees were starting to show signs of life. A friend of mine informed me that all the Jews in

Thessaloniki had been expelled from their homes and sent to a concentration camp in Poland. All the Jews in Athens were required to register at the City Hall. If we did not register, we would not have cards for food rations. Many of my family and friends were the last to be lured into registering.

In March 1944, a week before Passover, we were asked to report to our synagogue to receive flour to make matzah for our holiday. Many Jews wanted to remain outside the synagogue, but German soldiers herded us in and slammed the door shut. We hardly had room to breathe, but every so often the door opened and more captured Jews were shoved in. The synagogue was overflowing with people. The SS, with machine guns in their hands, faced the petrified crowd. Now I began to feel the meaning of anti-Semitism. My eyes searched for familiar faces and fell upon those of my two brothers-in-law and two nephews, David, twelve years old, and Joseph, eighteen years old. A few hours later, with armed German soldiers carefully guarding us, we were loaded into trucks.

On the way to Haidari, outside Athens, I felt a gentle but trembling young hand reaching for mine. It was my nephew David, crying. He held my hand and would not let go during the whole journey. Finally we reached a large, bare barracks. No one gave us any food. That night David and I lay down on the cold tile floor amidst hundreds of people and fell asleep.

As I opened my eyes, and saw the Nazis shoving mothers carrying babies and sick old men barely able to walk, I knew it wasn't a dream. It was real. Finally the Nazis gave us a meager portion of food. Swallowing my few bites, I felt relieved that my wife and child were not here and hoped they were safe. Confused and bewildered, people were telling each other that there must have been a mistake and in a few days we would go home. I wanted to believe them, but deep down I knew that the Nazis had not brought us here just to let us go again.

David never left my sight. He wept and shook with fear whenever he saw the SS. Each day the barracks became more dirty, and David was covered with lice. We had no drinking water, let alone water for washing. As I looked at David, he said, "Do you think rainwater would get rid of my lice?" I thought how good it would feel to walk in the rain. In my mind's eye I could picture my wife boiling the water to make me a cup of tea or opening the ice box and pouring me a cold glass of water. Somehow I had never before realized how important water was and how much I would miss it. I wondered if I would ever shave again as I watched the people around me becoming more dirty and emaciated. Did I look like them? No matter what, I could not give up hope.

A Tragic Journey

On April 2, we were taken to a train station, put into groups of sixty, and crowded into freight cars. Each of us was given a bucket to serve as a toilet. We wondered where we were going and how long the journey would last. It was difficult to see outside because there was only one small window and the whole freight car became dark. The train stopped. People from the Red Cross were given permission by the SS to give us food and cigarettes. I looked into the faces of the volunteers and hoped that these civilized people would tell the world

Loading the boxcars.

what they had seen, of the injustice being done to the Jews. This was only a false hope because the freight train then started moving again towards its destination.

Hours passed, the smell became unbearable. The lice spread to all of us, and weak people, one by one, were dying. One of them was my old teacher, whom I loved very much. When I was able to look out of the small window I could see the beautiful villages. Farmers were picking fruits from their trees, and I wondered if I would ever again taste a juicy apple or drink fresh orange juice. I envied the people enjoying the fresh air of spring and remembered how I used to lie on the grass and bake in the sun. I could not understand why I had been locked up without having done harm to anyone. I despaired and began to weep like a baby. After a week or so, the train stopped in an unknown country. The dead bodies were taken out and buried. The meager food of stale bread and limp carrots was running out, and with it, my strength. David grew thin and withered. The only comfort I could give him was to lie close to him, with my arms around his frail body, and talk to him. The train continued on its way. Weeks passed and I was sure we were crossing into Eastern Europe.

Auschwitz

On April 24, 1944, the great doors of the freight train finally opened and we were ordered to get out. My body, as weak and bent as the others, was forced out merely by the desire to see the daylight and smell the fresh air. My eyes were blinded temporarily by the sun, but the air that I smelled had a pungent aroma. I thought my senses were numb, but somehow I could feel the danger when I heard that we were at Auschwitz in Poland.

As we huddled together, the SS quickly separated the men from the women. They took the old and the sick and put them in a special line. They asked for twins, but no one volunteered, even though there were twins among us. The doctor who examined me had a pen-like instrument in his hand that marked me for life. He held my arm down on a table and tattooed it with the

69

number 182699. My entire body was shaved, then I was given a shower and afterwards was issued clothes that had huge red painted marks on them. This was so I could be easily spotted as a prisoner if I tried to escape. Now I found myself in a quarantine camp with hundreds of other innocent people. The camp consisted of blocks and blocks of barracks. I was very hungry because they had not fed us for two days. When the SS finally gave us a piece of bread, I devoured it like a wolf.

I met another Greek man who had been in Auschwitz for some time. He showed me thirty-six large cellblocks, and in each one of them there were three or four hundred prisoners. I told him about my nephew, David, and wondered where he was. The man just pointed towards a large chimney with huge flames coming out of it. Laughing bitterly, he said, "Those flames are human bodies." My body became a piece of ice. I couldn't feel a thing. Were the SS really so inhuman? The man saw how upset I was and said, "You'll get used to it."

Every morning, along with the other prisoners, I was awakened at 5 o'clock and taken to work. Watched by the SS, we hauled wheelbarrows full of stones from one place to another. Some of the workers were beaten mercilessly by the SS for not working fast enough. During all of this the German guards laughed viciously. I realized that some people can laugh out of despair and others laugh sadistically. For lunch I received a small amount of soup, and for dinner four of us shared a loaf of bread and a little bit of water, dirty and filled with rust. After two weeks I landed in the hospital.

Sickness and Mitzvah

Sitting on my bed, I noticed a German doctor and three SS soldiers entering the hospital. Someone quickly whispered to me to hide under my bed. From my hiding place I watched as the Germans grabbed the sick, beating them and dragging them off in a truck. A French doctor, also a prisoner, secretly gave me double rations of food and helped to get me out of the hospital. As I left,

The Nazi death camp of Auschwitz. Thousands of Jews were gassed, shot, and burned to death here.

this friend advised me to have courage and self-control in order to get through the dangers and difficulties that would be facing me.

Back at work I used all my strength to pull the wheelbarrow. To stop would be to invite the SS to beat or hit me. One day, sitting on a rock eating my meager lunch, I saw from afar a large group of children walking with German dogs guarding them. I could not take another bite and just sat there watching silently, wondering if my David was with them. These precious children were walking, talking, and even laughing despite their separation from their parents and friends.

With each passing day I became more apathetic and indifferent, knowing that the Germans were killing up to ten thousand people daily. The horror of Auschwitz no longer made any impression on me. I resembled a robot, caring only for myself,

stealing and lying to survive. Trying to escape meant a death sentence. The camp was surrounded by electrified barbed wire, bloodhounds, huge searchlights, and guards carrying machine guns. Yet I joined a group who made plans to escape.

With the coming of summer I became weaker, and I noted that fewer and fewer people were coming to work. By September, the heat turned to constant rain. As I watched the rain clouds drift away, I wondered if the dark clouds in my life would also disappear. News reached us that the Germans were losing the war. The frequent sound of air raid sirens and the aggitated behavior of the SS gave me some hope.

I joined a revolt against the Nazis guards even though I knew there might be informers in our group. I felt that I would rather die fighting for my freedom than be led, helplessly, into a gas chamber. As I had

71

anticipated, we were betrayed, and many of the group were tortured and killed before our eyes. Months passed and a deep depression came over me. My mind was a blank and my body had no more strength. In this condition, I was taken to be examined by a German doctor. Standing with others in line, we knew that we could not pass the examination and this would be our death sentence. All of a sudden I saw a guard turn away for a moment. In that second, I moved into the line of those who had been checked and passed for work.

Frozen Limbs

Our group was sent to Breslau in Germany, where it was snowy and cold. I stood outside in the snow, wearing only thin ragged clothes and wooden clogs on my feet, without socks. We worked at hard labor for twelve hours a day in the snow. This went on for a few months. When we slipped while walking in the snow, falling out of our wooden clogs, the German guards would beat us. Despite my frozen, numb feet, I dug ditches for water pipes. My frozen hands were barely able to hold the pickax, but I still scrapped away at the dirt. It was continually snowing and the ditches filled with mud, making the job harder. The only food that my soaked body received was two bowls of cabbage and an eighth of a loaf of bread. We worked in a temperature of 28 degrees below freezing. Fortunately, we had a few days off when the guards refused to watch us. Despite their warm fires, they were unwilling to stand outside in the cold.

By January 17 my entire body was frozen and covered with sores. I was sent to the infirmary. My feet were black from frostbite. Refusing to let the doctors amputate some fingers and toes, I was sent to the camp section for people who were dying. I could only think of my wife and daughter. Could they be safe in hiding somewhere, or were they also suffering in a camp as I was? Everyday I recalled memories of my home and my friends.

Jews working in a forced labor camp.

The Opened Gates

On May 7, we heard shouts from our warden, a fellow Jew. Shaking even the dead, he screamed, "The Germans are gone, the gates are open, we are free!" Trying to get to the gate, I kept falling, and while some made it out of the camp, I did not. Someone took sugar from the storehouse and brought it to us. Crawling on my knees, I took a handful and ate it like a maniac. I did not have any water to drink. Wrapped in dirt, I watched as two Russian soldiers raised their flag on the camp gates. I felt someone staring

72

at me as if I were some sort of strange, unbelievable object. I looked like a skeleton rather than a man. He asked, "Are you all right?" "I'm hungry," I whispered. "I haven't eaten for days." Within a short time he brought me bread, sausage, and cigarettes. I gorged myself with the bread and sausage, only to feel weak and dizzy. I watched my friends die from overeating. Doctors warned us to be careful and not eat too much. Many did not listen. We were taken to a hospital, where we were deloused and given baths for the first time in several years. Weighing 32 kilos (70 pounds), I was carried and put into a bed that had crisp, clean sheets that reminded me of my home. As I was being cared for, I wondered whether Athens looked the same, and whether my non-Jewish friends and customers ever worried about me. Despite the doctor's warning, I left the hospital to search for my family. Weak and unable to continue searching, I was again taken to a hospital, an American hospital, filled with prisoners of war.

On August 25, 1945, along with many other Greek Jews, I boarded the *Queen Elizabeth*, the ship that would take us home to Greece. When it anchored off Athens, refusing to leave the deck, I looked across the harbor at the beautiful city and felt near to my home, yet still far away. Confused and upset, I wondered if my family would recognize me. A small boat took me ashore. When it landed I saw people searching for their relatives. I heard a familiar voice calling my name. It was my wife and my little daughter; they hugged me continuously. Now my dreams came true. On the way home, I looked down at my arm and there I saw my number.

Darkness in the Synagogue

Something to Think About

The author's life was saved when someone whispered to him to hide under his bed. Later, a French doctor helped him survive by giving him double rations of food. These are examples of a value called in Hebrew *piku'ah nefesh*, which means that we each have a duty to save a human life when it is imperiled. This duty is based on Leviticus 19:16, "neither shall you stand by your neighbor's blood."

Voices from Tradition

Only one single man was created in the world, to teach that if any man has caused a single soul to perish, Scripture considers it to him as though he had caused a whole world to perish, and if any man saves a single soul, Scripture credits it to him as though he had saved a whole world. Again, but a single man was created for the sake of peace among mankind, that none should say to his fellow, "My father was greater than your father"; also, that unbelievers should not say, "There are many ruling powers in heaven." Again, but a single man was created to proclaim the greatness of God, for man stamps many coins with one die, and they are all like to one another; but God has stamped every man with the die of the first man, yet not one of them is like his fellow. Therefore every one must say, "For my sake was the world created."

— Mishnah (Sanhedrin 4:5)

On the Shabbat one is required to save the soul of a Jew and a gentile alike.
— Babylonian Talmud (Yoma 85a)

And in Your Opinion...

1. In the passage from Sanhedrin, much is made of all of us coming from a single original ancestor. Do you think that is why Judaism teaches that we have a duty to save any and all human life?

2. In the story, the section that takes place in the hospital is called, "Sickness and Mitzvah." The meaning of "Sickness" is clear from the setting in the hospital. But what do you think is the mitzvah he is referring to?

Strength and Resistance

Arie Shnaper

On January 21, 1942, in a small communal kitchen in the Ghetto of Vilna, a group of us gathered, representing the General Zionists, Gordonia, Dror, the Revisionists, Hashomer Hatzair, the Bund, and the Communists. All of us, though members of different youth groups, were united in our belief in a Jewish State. We sometimes differed on how to achieve it, but we were all inspired by a shared understanding of our biblical past. The purpose of our meeting was to honor the memory of the Jews who had been murdered in nearby Ponar by the Nazis. We issued the following statement: "Let us not be led like sheep to the slaughter. Of the 80,000 Jews in Vilna, only 20,000 remain. Our parents, brothers, and sisters have been wrested from us before our eyes. Where are the hundreds of men seized by the town police for work? Where are the innocent women and children who were taken on that horrible night of persecution? Where are the Jews who were captured on Yom Kippur, and where are our brothers from the smaller Ghetto? Those who were taken out of the Ghetto will never return, because all roads to Ponar mean death. Hitler plans to systematically annihilate all Jews. First to go are the Jews of Europe. Though we are weak, without guns, grenades, and explosives, our only honorable answer to the enemy is: resistance!"

At the end of December 1942, the same group met again, to officially form the United Partisan Organization. By this time the Germans had already murdered 50,000 Jews

in Ponar, which was 15 kilometers from Vilna. We had three major objectives: to obtain arms, to wage acts of sabotage against the Germans whenever possible, and most important of all, to resist when the Germans began the final liquidation of the Ghetto. Then they would see that we were not like sheep to be led to our death.

Smuggled Weapons

It was extremely difficult to obtain arms. Many Jews paid with their lives when attempting to purchase or steal them. Even the smallest weapon was very expensive. Every member of our group donated something of value. I gave my last few coins for the cause.

A friend of mine was caught and killed by the SS while trying to buy a gun. The few weapons we were able to acquire were smuggled into the Ghetto through sewers and secret entrances. What joy I felt when I heard that the first grenade had been smuggled into the Ghetto. Our group, who were all young, met several times a week. We were not allowed to tell our families or even our closest friends about the organization. Since the Ghetto was very crowded, and several families lived together in each room, it was not easy to maintain secrecy. That first night, when I was told that I would have to learn to fight and use a gun, I realized that the struggle for life was worthwhile because it would give me a chance to protect Jewish life and Jewish honor.

It gave me strength to hear that despite all the difficulties, our sabotage efforts against the German war machine could succeed. Those of us who still were selected to work for the Germans were taken from the Ghetto in the morning and returned at night from our jobs of hard labor. I survived not on the meager food provided by the Germans, but on scraps found in garbage cans, fields, and wherever I could steal something. Outside the Ghetto, Jewish resistance fighters wrecked trains loaded with soldiers and ammunition on the way to the Eastern Front. Undaunted by the risk of being captured or killed, they carried out their missions and did whatever needed to be done.

Taking Risks

One evening, while we were in our little meeting room, one of my friends told the following story: "One day at the arsenal a young German holding a grenade in his hands became puzzled because this particular grenade looked unusual to him. He asked my friend, who was an engineer working at the arsenal, how the grenade worked. Taking advantage of this opportunity for sabotage, my friend yelled, 'Throw it away or you will be killed,' pointing in the direction of a huge pile of ammunition. The German did as he was advised. The grenade exploded and destroyed over a million and half bullets."

I too took risks. While working at the airport, whenever there was an opportunity, I would unscrew important parts of an airplane, or let the gasoline run out of a German tank, or throw a lit cigarette into the gasoline supply dump. Taking these risks gave me confidence and hope, for I knew that I and the other Ghetto fighters were protecting Jewish life and Jewish honor. Nevertheless, most of the Ghetto Jews felt that our actions would hasten the destruction of the Ghetto.

Hashomer Hatzair, 1925, Poland.

I remember one courier, Liza Magun, who brought us important news from other Ghetto fighters. She was caught, tortured, and killed, but she never revealed any secrets or our identities.

On July 16, 1943, the Gestapo arrested two important non-Jewish underground workers in the city who had been in contact with our United Partisan Organization. One of the prisoners revealed the name of our commander, a man named Wittenberg. The Gestapo demanded his surrender. The Ghetto Jews wanted him to surrender because they were afraid that the whole Ghetto would be destroyed. The prewar Jewish underworld of the Ghetto marched to the headquarters of the United Partisan Organization and attacked us, the Ghetto fighters, with sticks and iron rods. The fighters answered with fire, and my hands trembled when I had to use my gun against fellow Jews instead of the Germans. Our leader, who did not want brother to kill brother, surrendered to the Nazis. He was tortured and killed but did not betray any of the Ghetto fighters. A

friend of mine, Aba Kovner of Hashomer Hatzair, became the successor of Wittenberg. He survived and is now in Israel, living on a kibbutz where he is an important poet.

The Fall of the Ghetto

At the end of April 1943, news of the Warsaw Ghetto uprising reached the Vilna Ghetto through the underground radio from England. The Warsaw Ghetto was in flames and the Germans were now destroying it. It was a sad, sad day. I asked myself, "Is this the end, is our end approaching?" Then, at this time, Hirshken Glick answered my question by writing the song, "Zog net Keinmel 'as du gaist dem letzten veg" ("Never say that you are going the last path"), which became the anthem of the Jewish Partisans.

On August 1, 1943, I stopped going to work. A few days later the Germans announced that there would be work if we came to register. The labor office in the Ghetto had a long line of Jews waiting for registration. I did not go. I knew better. The

waiting Jews were surrounded by the Gestapo, Ukrainians, and Estonians and forced onto freight cars. They resisted and fought with bare hands against the armed host, killing quite a few of them. Three hundred Jews were killed, and the rest were sent to Estonia for "work."

On September 1, 1943, at dawn, the Ghetto was surrounded by Germans, Estonians, Lithuanians, and Ukrainians. I went to my fighting post and my friends went to theirs. Several Germans were killed in the battle that followed. One of our outposts was burned by the Germans. The post where I was stationed was surrounded and forty of us were captured. We were taken away by truck. On the way to the station, where we were supposed to board a train for Estonia, we decided to attempt an escape. I was the first to jump off the truck, but no one followed me because the German guards were able to stop the others. Although I got away from the Germans, I was caught by the Polish police and handed over to the Lithuanian police, who brought me to the train. I was sent on the transport to Estonia with the others.

The whole Vilna Ghetto was liquidated on September 23, 1943. A few of the remaining resistance fighters escaped through the sewers into the forests. One hundred and fifty members of the United Partisan Organization survived after the destruction of the Vilna Ghetto.

Abba Kovner was one of the commanders of the Vilna Ghetto and helped organize the armed revolt. After his escape he continued to fight the Germans as the leader of Jewish partisan groups in the Vilna forest. After the war he immigrated to Israel, where he became a famous Hebrew poet.

Jewish partisans from Vilna who fought in the forests.

Strength and Resistance

Something to Think About

In the story we learn that the Gestapo demanded the surrender of an underground commander and he surrendered to certain death in order to protect the rest of the Jewish community. His name was Wittenberg. Was Wittenberg a martyr? Should he have done what he did? What do you think about the community's behavior in that part of the story?

Voices from Tradition

The historian Josephus tells us that Eliezer ben Yair led the Jews on Masada, at the end of the great Jewish rebellion of the first century of the common era, to take their own lives rather than be captured and made slaves by the Romans.

Modern rabbinic authorities differ on whether a person must sacrifice himself as Wittenberg did. Rabbi A. I. Kook said, yes, martyrdom is obligatory if it saves the community. Other rabbis have taught that although martyrdom is laudatory and meritorious, it is not mandatory.

When Akiba was being tortured, the hour for saying the Shema arrived. He said it and smiled. The Roman officer called out, "Old man, are you a sorcerer, or do you mock your sufferings, that you smile in the midst of your pain?" "Neither," replied Akiba, "but all my life, when I said the words, 'Thou shalt love the Lord thy God with all thy heart and soul and might,' I was saddened, for I thought, when shall I be able to fulfill the command? I have loved God with all my heart and with all my possessions (might), but how to love God with all my soul (i.e., my life) was not assured to me. Now that I am giving my life, and that the hour for saying the Shema has come, and my resolution remains firm, should I not laugh?" And as he spoke, his soul departed.

— Jerusalem Talmud (Berachot 9:7)

And in your Opinion...

In the quote from the Talmud above, we learn how Rabbi Akiba was willing (even anxious) to give up his life out of his love for God. Our tradition understands and approves of that kind of martyrdom under those circumstances. However, the Rabbis never accepted the martyrdom of Eleazer ben Yair and those at Masada as a model for Jews. Why do you think that is? Could it be that their martyrdom, which denied the Romans, did not save the community from death. Which kind of martyr was Wittenberg in the story? To help you with this, you may want to write a speech for your class. The goal would be to convince the others that Akiba is the better model for Jewish behavior, or that Eleazer is, depending on your point of view.

Zivia Lubetkin

"Your Salvation Lies In Fighting"
part I

Who was Adolph Eichmann?

Adolph Eichmann was the chief of operations in the Nazi scheme to exterminate European Jewry. He headed the Department for Jewish Affairs at Gestapo headquarters until the collapse of the Third Reich.

At the end of the war, Eichmann was captured and imprisoned, but in 1950 he escaped to Argentina. He and his family lived in Buenos Aires under fictitious names.

In 1960 he was kidnapped by the Israelis and secretly flown to Israel to stand trial for his crimes. More than 100 volumes of testimony (Zivia Lubetkin) and some 1600 documents from German archives were presented at the trial. The court found that he was the central figure in carrying out the "Final Solution."

Eichmann was found guilty and sentenced to death. He was hanged and his body cremated.

The following testimony was presented by Zivia Lubetkin at Adolph Eichmann's trial.

Who was Zivia Lubetkin?

At the time of the Warsaw ghetto uprising (April, 1943) Zivia Lubetkin was among the organizers and the combatants. When the ghetto was conquered she and her companions escaped through the sewer system. Zivia and the other survivors continued the fight with the Polish partisans.

In July, 1944 Zivia immigrated to Palestine. She and her husband Yitzhak Zuckerman founded the kibbutz Lohammay Ha'Getta (Fighters of the Ghetto).

This is a shortened version of her testimony at the Eichmann trial.

IN THE DISTRICT COURT OF JERUSALEM
Criminal Case No. 40/61

Before:
> THEIR HONOURS,
> > The Presiding Judge: MOSHE LANDAU
> > Judge: BENJAMIN HALEVI
> > Judge: YITZHAK RAVEH

SESSION NO. 25

Date:	3.5.1961
Secretary:	JOSEPH BODENHEIMER:
FOR THE PROSECUTION:	The Attorney-General of the Government of Israel
	GIDEON HAUSNER: Solicitor-General
	GAVRIEL BACH: Deputy
	YA'AKOV ROBINSON:
FOR THE DEFENSE:	DR. ROBERT SERVATIUS

IN THE DISTRICT COURT OF JERUSALEM
Criminal Case No. 40/61

**THE ATTORNEY-GENERAL
OF THE GOVERNMENT OF ISRAEL**

v.

**ADOLF, THE SON OF
ADOLF KARL EICHMANN**

MINUTES OF SESSION NO. 25

Presiding Judge: Mrs. Lubetkin, please put your right hand on the Bible and repeat after me.

Witness Lubetkin: I swear by God that my testimony in this trial will be the truth, the whole truth, and nothing but the truth.

Attorney-General: You are a member of Kibbutz Lohamei ha-Getta'ot (Ghetto Fighters Collective Village).

Presiding Judge: What is your full name?

Witness Lubetkin: Zivia Lubetkin Zuckerman.

Attorney-General: Are you the wife of Yitzhak Zuckerman?

A. Yes.

Q. In the summer of 1939 you went to the Zionist Congress in Geneva, and at the beginning of September, 1939, you returned to Warsaw?

A. Yes.

Q. You were then working with the Hechalutz Pioneer Movement?

A. At the Hechalutz Center in Warsaw.

Attorney-General: Later you left Warsaw? You crossed the Soviet border at the beginning of January, 1940 — and when did you return to Warsaw?

Witness Lubetkin-Zuckerman: At the beginning of January, 1940.

Q. What did you see when you returned to Warsaw?

A. When I came to Warsaw, I found that many new directives and laws had been issued against the Jews. The order about the wearing of the yellow badge — the Magen David. The marking of Jewish shops with a Magen David. A prohibition of medical aid — Jewish doctors were prohibited from treating non-Jewish patients, and vice-versa.

For instance, during the first days of the ghetto, a Polish policeman was looking for a Jew to avenge himself. The Jew drew a pistol and killed the Polish policeman. And then, the following morning, Germans entered the house at 9 Vialeski Street and arrested 50 of the Jewish residents, as well as some others who were there by accident. They were taken, and we never saw them again. This was done to intimidate the Jews and teach them a lesson. Another hardship was the seizure of people off the streets for forced labor. When a man left his house, he never knew if he would come back and when.

Attorney-General: You also dealt with the smuggling of food, didn't you?

Witness Lubetkin: Yes, we smuggled food. Although I must say now that there were professionals in this branch of our activities. One of the problems was, and there is no doubt that this was a national enterprise — a human enterprise of the first degree, a holy enterprise, to smuggle food into the ghetto.

Q. And when people were caught at the gates with smuggled food, what happened to them?

A. Of course smuggling was really done in different ways. First and foremost, by bribing the Germans; and no German formation, not even the Gestapo, ever refused Jewish money. And by paying bribes one could smuggle food into the ghetto. But of course sometimes the Germans took the bribes, and then the guards were changed, and the new guards were not the same ones who got the money, and if the Jews were late — sometimes only a matter of ten minutes — since the guard had been changed, they paid for it with their lives.

Q. Did children ever pass through the gates to the Aryan part of the city?

A. During the very difficult periods of hunger, there were whole families where the breadwinners were children between the ages of seven and eleven, because the age of twelve in the ghetto was already considered an adult person.

Q. How did they manage to win their bread?

A. Groups of children used to gather near the gates, waiting for an opportunity when the German would turn his back to light a cigarette, and then masses of them would cross over to the Aryan side. The Germans would always pursue and shoot at those children. Some of the children were always killed.

Presiding Judge: Where were you sent to Warsaw? Where from?

Witness: From Kobel — a town which was under Soviet rule.

Q. Is that the town you were born in?

A. No — I was born in the district of Beten. I left my parents there, but I was in Kobel with a group of friends. We went to Warsaw, and started activities. We sent people to Vilna, so that they could go on to Israel — because there was still a kind of opening. The second aim of my mission was to encourage Jews to leave the area occupied by the Germans and escape to Lithuania. At that time

Youthful smugglers scaling the walls of the Warsaw Ghetto.

The wall around the Ghetto was built with Jewish money. The Jewish Council paid a German construction firm for the materials and the building costs. Sharp pieces of glass and razor sharp barbed wire were set into the wall to prevent escapes.

there were rumors — and it was true — that many of them could be saved. Some of them are now in Israel. And it was still possibile to get people from Lithuania to Palestine at the time.

I came to the house at 34 Jzana Street, this was where the Merkaz HaHalutz had conducted its activities before the war. When we, the former residents, were ordered to leave and move eastwards, this house soon filled up with people coming to Warsaw. When I returned here, I found 180 young boys and girls in the home, and they were not alone. During the air-raids, they shared one glass of water. And, if one of them found one potato, he would share it with six comrades. And since places existed in all youth movements in Warsaw — there were some five or six such centers — these were in the centers where the best and the flower of our youth was organized, and reached Warsaw. In the beginning when the ghetto was open and people were allowed to travel, we made contacts outside the ghetto. When the ghetto was sealed off, we searched for new ways.

Q. And of course Jewish life was going on underground, and you organized an underground movement representing all the various political shades?

A. Right from the beginning, the main activity was organizational. We called on all the youth movements to organize. They all responded, from the far right parties to the leftist.

Q. Please excuse me. Were secular movements and religious movements included?

90

A. Yes, all movements were included. I remember, for instance, the first meeting, and I was present at the meeting. This was in 1941, a short time before the ghetto was set up. Dozens of young people, boys and girls, came from twenty-four towns in Poland and spent three weeks in Chelna hungry and freezing, studying. And the value of this program was very important to the pupils and to the teachers.

These pupils would then go out to the towns in Poland and bring our word to the Jews there, encouraging them, teaching them to resist the persecutors, organizing the young people in their own town and of course, this was one of the things — we would protect the image of God that had been given us.

Attorney General: In June, 1941, war broke out between Germany and the Soviet Union. How did it affect Jewish life in the ghettoes?

A. At the beginning, it was a kind of encouragement. The Jews somehow believed that the Russians would advance, beat the Germans, and perhaps this would mean the end of the war. On the whole it is not difficult to understand — when a man is in trouble he grasps at straws — maybe, perhaps. I was not one of the optimists in the ghetto.

Q. You established relationships with the People's Army?

A. We tried to make connections with the Polish underground. But at the time they were only beginning to organize, and the Polish underground was still not taking action, not fighting back. This underground was mainly busy organizing, encouraging, but at this time they had not yet taken up arms.

Q. Will you tell the court about Hanech?

A. In the meantime the Germans advanced, and as you know, they conquered huge areas populated by many Jews, like Vilna, Lithuania, and Galicia — they were all populated, densely populated, by Jews. As the army advanced, we decided to set up contacts with Jewish centers in those places.

We decided for the first time to send a Pole by the name of Henneck. He was a member of the Polish scouts, with whom we had contact from the first day, Hanech was sent to Vilna. We did not know what was happening there — how the Jews were faring, the organizational situation. He was given addresses. There was a great concentration of Jewish youth in Vilna, preparing to go to

The first proclamation by the German commander of the Vilna Ghetto: "The German soldiers have come to free the population from Communist bondage. The Jews must wear arm bands with a Star of David; they must not leave their quarters; they must carry out their required work and surrender their radios."

Israel, and we knew that not all of them had gotten away. And hundreds of *halutzim* remained behind because the roads were closed.

The journey to Vilna took a few months because between Warsaw and Vilna there were three borders to cross, three frontiers — an area annexed to the Reich, and then the Baltic countries, another frontier — and even a Pole, a Gentile Pole, had to be very brave as well as very lucky to be able to cross those frontiers.

"Your Salvation Lies In Fighting"
part II

Attorney-General: Where was your base of operations?

Witness Lubetkin: Outside Warsaw we had a farm, Sinyakov, and besides providing a means of livelihood, this farm was also a kind of springboard for those who acted as our emissaries and messengers outside the ghetto. We worked for a Polish farmer as Jews. And our emissaries and messengers were walking the Aryan streets in Warsaw and every moment endangered their lives because they might be recognized as Jewish. When we had this base to which one could come in the evening, to this farm to be with friends and to be Jewish openly, this was something very important. We kept our papers and pamphlets there, and then we had a call from Czenyakov that Hanech had arrived and that we were to come to a meeting. We were very glad; we still had various ways to leave the ghetto in spite of the excellent guards. Of course, when we left the ghetto we would remove the Magen David and go about the streets as Aryans. It was in the evening, there was no electricity, and Hanech told his story. For the first time we heard that Jews of Vilna were being deported by the thousands and tens of thousands, and being killed, children and women.

Fifty Jewish combat groups — a thousand men and women armed with eighty rifles, three light machine guns, a few hundred revolvers, and a thousand hand grenades — put up a desperate fight against two thousand members of the occupying forces under SS General Stroop, who had been ordered to destroy the Warsaw Ghetto.

Attorney-General: And then you knew that this would be your fate as well?

A. This was at the end of 1941. Early in 1942, a Jew escaped from Chelmno and came to Warsaw. He told us that in Chelmno Jews were being taken out of town in trucks and killed with poison gas.

Q. Did you believe him?

General Jurgen von Stroop, the German commanding officer during the Warsaw Ghetto uprising.

A. When the Jew reached Warsaw, he told the story to a rabbi. The rabbi swore that the man was out of his mind. He did not believe him. But when we heard the story about Vilna, and then the story about Chelmno, we believed that this was the system and this was the plan.

Q. How did you react to this news?

A. We put all the stories together and when we heard from Hanech, we stopped all cultural activities. We closed the Hebrew Gymnasium, the dramatic troupes and concentrated all our efforts on active defense. But the Jews did not believe! Why didn't they believe? The answer is very simple. It was hard to believe. It was hard to imagine that a whole nation could be exterminated.

Q. What happened on Yom Kippur of 1942?

A. The Jewish police, who were so confident of their own safety because they were loyal to the Germans — they were not spared. They too were taken to Treblinka. On the Day of Atonement, 1942, out of half a million Jews there had been in Warsaw, only sixty thousand remained within the ghetto walls.

    In the meantime, the Jewish Fighting Organization was set up.

Witness Lubetkin: Mordecai Anielewicz headed it, this organization.

Attorney-General: And your husband, Zuckerman, was his assistant.

Q. Will you please tell the Court what happened in April '43 before Easter, before Pesach.?

A. The 18th of April, 1943, was the day before Pesach. Two days earlier the Gestapo man Brund walked into the Community Council office and said that the Council was not providing adequate care for the Jewish children. There was not enough food and not enough vegetables, and he suggested that kindergartens should be set up so the Jewish children could play and laugh, because he was certain that those Jews who remained in Warsaw were productive and there was no danger of deportation. By now we were experienced, and we knew that whenever there were rumors and promises of this kind, it was a bad omen.

Q. Did you believe him?

A. On the 18th a Jewish policeman who was a member of the underground organization reported that the Polish policemen had told the Jewish policemen that they did not know exactly when, but something would happen tonight. Of course, we, the Jewish Fighting Organization, which had fighting units throughout the ghetto, and each group had its post, we declared a state of readiness. Everyone was to man his post. And around midnight, this policeman came and told us the ghetto had been surrounded.

Q. Please continue.

A. We separated, and I went to the post at 33 Nalewki Street, and the commander of that group was Zachariah Auster. The other comrades, Anielewicz and others, went to their posts. Mordecai Anielewicz went to 29 Miller Street. What did we say to the Jews on that night? We said: "He who has arms will fight," and we did have arms — not only the Fighting Organization but Jews who did not belong to the organization. And we said, "He who has no arms, women and children, will go down into the bunkers. And at the first opportunity during the chaos of the fighting, let them go to the Aryan side. Go to the woods. Some of them will be saved." And of course to the fighting groups we said we did not have to issue orders. For months these young men and young women had been waiting for the moment when they would be able to shoot Germans. And the moment arrived.

Q. What happened then?

A. Morning came, I was standing in the attic at 23 Nalewki Street, and I saw thousands of Germans surrounding the ghetto with machine guns. And all of a sudden they started entering the ghetto, thousands armed as if they were going to the front against Russia. And we, some twenty men and women, young. And what were our arms? The arms we had — we had a revolver, a grenade, and a whole group had two guns, and some bombs, home-made, prepared in a very primitive way. We had to light them with matches, and Molotov cocktails. It was strange to see those twenty men and women, Jewish men and women, standing up against the armed great enemy, glad and merry, because we knew that their end would come. We knew that they would defeat us, but they would pay a high price for our lives. And it is difficult to explain. Many of you will not believe this, but when the Germans came up to our posts and marched by, and we threw those hand grenades and bombs, and saw German blood flowing over the streets of Warsaw after we had seen so much Jewish blood running in the streets of Warsaw before that, there was rejoicing. Tomorrow did not worry us. The Jewish fighters rejoiced to see the wonder and the miracle — those German "heroes" retreating!

Attorney General: Continue!

I remember the second day of the uprising — it was Pesach. In one of the bunkers I met a rabbi, Rabbi Meisel. We had connections with him, the underground, also on ordinary days. The underground had not always been helped and encouraged by the Jewish people. It was not always well received. Some people thought we endangered the life of the Jewish community there, the collective responsibility — the terror the Germans had succeeded in arousing among the Jewish people. And when I came into the bunker, the rabbi interrupted the Seder ceremony and said, "You are welcome. I die a happier man now. I wish we had done this earlier."

May every house become a fortress! Rise up, people, and fight!!! Your salvation lies in fighting! He who fights for his life has the chance of saving himself! We rise up in the name of the fight for the lives of the helpless whom we wish to save and whom we must rouse to action!

From an underground leaflet

And thus the fighting continued for days. From the very first day we were looking for contacts on the Aryan side. We had a number of friends — Yitzhak Zuckerman among them — on the Aryan side. There was the problem of additional arms, and after some time he succeeded in getting hold of arms. But the question was how to smuggle the arms into the ghetto. We had telephone communication at the time, via the men of the Burial Society. Our cemetery was outside the ghetto walls, and since the men of the burial group were over-worked — they always had to leave the ghetto and come back — thus we received arms. We heard from Zuckerman that he had gotten hold of a number of guns and they would be smuggled in within a few days. We also sent letters outside the ghetto through the men on the burial unit, and we sent a letter from Mordecai Anielewicz. And then this contact was also cut off.

Q. How did you reestablish contact?

A. We sent two comrades to make contacts with our comrades on the Aryan side — Simcha Ratheiser, now in Jerusalem, and another one, who is dead. And when they reached the Aryan side and the Polish guard saw them, he thought they were Poles, and said, "Do you know what happened here an hour ago?" and he told them about the fighting which had taken place an hour before they came.

Q. When you began the uprising, did you know how it would end? Did you have any hope of defeating the German Army?

A. No, we didn't have a fighting chance. That was clear. It was in April, 1943. There were only the first beginnings of the Russian victory on the front, and it was quite clear to us that we had no prospect of winning in the accepted sense of the word, the military sense of the word or the more accepted sense of the word — victory. But believe me, and this is not just rhetoric, in spite of their strength, we did know that eventually and finally we would be the winners. We, the weak ones, because that was our strength, our belief. We believed in justice, in man, in a way of life totally different than the one they stand for.

Q. When did you cross into the Aryan part of town?

A. It was on the 8th day of May.

Q. How did you cross?

Presiding Judge: Which year?

Witness Lubetkin: The 8th day of May, 1943, when the headquarters bunker of the organization was destroyed where Mordecai Anielewicz, the commander, was also hiding, and about twenty other fighters. It was just an accident that I was not there, because the previous day I had been sent on a mission to another part of the ghetto. When I returned I found no traces of the bunker and no people. There was only a small group of fighters who had managed to escape through some roundabout way — I don't know how — They told us what had happened. That night we decided — there were only a few of us left, no food, no water, hardly any arms, no ammunition for our pistols and for the few rifles which we did have — we decided to send a group of people into the sewers to try and cross over to the Aryan side and see what they could do. On their way through the sewers these comrades met a group of our people. One of them was Simcha Rotter, who had gone out to Milanowska. The group had been sent by our comrades, our friends on the Aryan side, together with a Polish man as a guide. They had come to bring us the surviving fighters through the sewers to the Aryan side. So I also joined them. For about 48 hours we wandered through the maze of sewers on the 12th of May. The underground wanted to help us but could not, only very few people could help us.

Q. How did you escape?

A. When our comrades realized that no help was coming, they simply hired two trucks and said they had to move some furniture. When they reached the street where we were standing inside the sewers, our friends whipped out pistols, pointed them at the driver, and said "These are not pieces of furniture — they are men, if you make one sound you will endanger their lives." And these people kept silent. They opened the manhole covers and we came out. I think we were about 50 fighters, and we climbed on the trucks. We went through the

Mordecai Anielewicz helped organize the revolt against the Nazis in the Warsaw Ghetto. He died fighting the Germans. This statue in memory of Mordecai Anielewicz is at Kibbutz Yad Mordecai in Israel.

streets of Warsaw, the busy daytime streets of Warsaw, arms in hand, until we reached a forest about seven kilometers from Warsaw. We really had nowhere to go.

Attorney-General: Yes, let's go on. You hid in Warsaw and you also fought when Polish Warsaw revolted, is that true?

Witness Lubetkin: Yes, together with the remnants of the Jewish Fighting Organization. We had a special group which fought with the Polish underground.

Q. Was that in August 1944?

A. Yes.

Q. And then that uprising was suppressed?

A. When that uprising was suppressed and the Poles decided to surrender and go into captivity, our group did not do so. For lack of any other alternative, we stayed in a bunker in the city of Warsaw, and I now mean Aryan Warsaw. There was no longer any Jewish Warsaw. Even in the Aryan areas it was no longer permitted, even Poles were no longer permitted, to exist there. Thus we entered a house which had a cellar. A group of Jewish fighters with their arms in hand, we entered this house, and we actually did not know what to do until we sent out a few girls to seek communications with the Aryan side. They did establish contact. They brought back a delegation from the Red Polish Army, and we told them that there were sick people here, people suffering from typhoid. The fighters among us who had characteristically Jewish faces were wrapped in bandages as though they were very ill and wounded, ... and they took us out under disguised as patients — typhoid patients — and we went across to the Aryan side to a township near Warsaw, and there we were when the Soviet Army liberated Warsaw in the middle of January, 1945.

Attorney-General: Thank you.

Presiding Judge: Dr. Servatius, have you any questions?

Dr. Servatius: I have no questions of this witness.

Presiding Judge: Thank you, Mrs. Lubetkin, you have concluded your testimony.

Attorney-General: Does the Court wish to have the recess now?

Presiding Judge: Is there any more lengthy testimony?

Attorney-General: No, it's not very long — about half an hour.

Presiding Judge: We shall now have a recess for twenty minutes.

"Your Salvation Lies In Fighting"

Something to Think About

In Zivia's testimony we learn how during particularly difficult periods children became the breadwinners for their families by risking their lives to cross over from the ghetto to the Aryan part of the city. Zivia makes a point of telling us how dangerous this was by saying, "There were always children who fell dead." What does our heritage teach us about the importance of children to Jews and Judaism? Below are what some sources say.

Voices from Tradition

Rabbi Judah said: "See how beloved the children are before God. When the Sanhedrin went into captivity, the Shechinah went not with them; the watchers of the priests went into captivity; the Shechinah went not with them. But when the children went into captivity, the Shechinah went with them. For it says in Lamentations 1:5, 'Her children are gone into captivity,' and immediately after (1:6), 'From Zion her splendor (God) is departed.'"

— Lamentations Rabbah (1:33)

When God was about to give the Torah to Israel, He asked them, "Will you accept my Torah?" and they answered, "We will." God said, "Give me surety that you will fulfill its ordinances." They said, "Let Abraham, Isaac, and Jacob be our pledges." God answered, "But the Patriarchs themselves need sureties..." Then Israel said, "Let the prophets be our sureties." God said, "But the prophets are insufficient." Then Israel said, "Let our children be our sureties." God said, "Such pledges will I indeed accept."

— Tanhuma (Vayiggash 2)

(Regarding schoolchildren studying the Book of Leviticus, much of which is about sacrifices), God said, "As the sacrifices are pure, so are the children pure."

— Pesihta Kahana (60b)

And in Your Opinion...

In her testimony, Zivia matter-of-factly describes the children's dangerous participation. Yet, the sources above regard children as an inestimable resource and treasure. Do you think the children should have been allowed to risk themselves as they did? Should they have been protected from such danger at all costs? Or, on the other hand, were matters so desperate that there was no other choice? Was the best chance for the children's survival for them to become the breadwinners as they did? Do you think under the circumstances their parents could have stopped them even if they had wished to? Did the circumstances require the children to act as and to be adults?

Dr. Leon Bass

A Black Soldier

My name is Leon Bass. I was born in Philadelphia in 1925 into a black family of five boys and one girl. My grandparents had lived on a farm in South Carolina, where my father was born in 1890, twenty-five years after the Emancipation Proclamation. My grandfather fought with the United States Army in the First World War. He was in Europe, and when he returned, he had a greater understanding of the Declaration of Independence. He was a changed man, but unfortunately the American people had not changed. Equality for black people was not to be seen or felt in the South for some time.

My grandparents were determined that all of their children would be educated in colleges and would learn that the land they lived in should belong to all people. So the Bass family left South Carolina and migrated to Philadelphia, never to take their children back to their birthplace.

I was very close to my grandfather. He believed in close family ties and felt that it was important for everyone in the family to help each other and help other people. He also explained to me the importance of being an educated person. I went to elementary and junior high school in West Philadelphia. My neighborhood was predominantly black. I did not encounter too much hatred or racism. Yet there were a few painful times when I was called "Nigger"

Leon Bass, the soldier.

and similar names by children who were strangers to me. I also knew that in some places there were different rules for blacks and whites. I, as a black child, could not sit with my white friends in a movie because the balcony, above, was for blacks. I remember going to a park where there was a pool and not being able to swim with the other children. I asked my parents why I couldn't swim in a public swimming pool. The answer was, "Blacks are not wanted." How painful it was to hear this, but I didn't know what to do about it. It was very frustrating, and I felt helpless. I had little power in a world dominated by whites.

My parents loved me and I loved them, but I grew up in a very sheltered, narrow environment, not knowing what it meant to be black. I wish that they had prepared me to cope as a minority in a prejudiced world. Every Sunday we used to get spruced up and my father took us to church. My mother remained at home. This was her day of rest. At home, organized religion did not play an important part, but I guess my parents wanted us to know that if we wished, desired, we could belong somewhere. We went to many different churches.

Segregation

In 1943, at the age of eighteen, I was drafted into the United States Army and was

Even the drivers' tests were segregated.

sent to Georgia for military training. I had heard about the South, and now, confronted with segregation and racism, what I had heard suddenly became very real to me. My battalion consisted of six hundred black soldiers; all of our officers were white. During orientation I was given the reasons why I had to fight for my country. It was for democracy and freedom. But what the officers preached, they did not practice. I watched their behavior and became a cynic. I knew I had to be silent because if I spoke out I would be punished.

What a shock it was to visit a nearby town in Georgia and see how everything was segregated. There were signs that said "For Colored Only" and "For Whites Only" on drinking fountains, in movies, and on buses. I felt powerless and wondered how I could help my people. How can you help others when you haven't any control over your own life? I felt weak and frustrated.

When I left Georgia I thought I knew what segregation really meant, but after spending time in Mississippi, I discovered the true meaning of segregation. One day, as I entered a bus, I was told to go and sit in the back. When I objected, an old black lady said to me, "Lordy, son, move or they'll kill you," and she meant it. I moved to the back, realizing that despite my military uniform, I was a black, had no special privileges. With each passing day I lost some of my dignity and pride. I recalled reading *Tom Sawyer* and *Huckleberry Finn*, and then Mark Twain's message about slavery and man's injustice to man became clear to me. I realized how even now there were very few "Hucks" ready to protect the rights of black people. My pain became more severe. I wondered, as people passed me by, how any black person could live in the South. I struggled with this real-life situation and wondered where the good people were to stop it.

In October 1944, I was shipped to England. On the way there I decided to read as many books as possible about slavery, bigotry, and its effect on people. I thought about my school, which by design was mostly black. The principal and the teachers were black. The only white people in my neighborhood were a white doctor, shopkeeper, tailor, and a few others. I remembered my two white school friends, one Italian and the other Jewish. The difference between us, I thought, was that they were white and I was black. A big surprise awaited me in England. Being treated as an equal was a wonderful and good feeling. After the South, this was quite an emotional experience for me.

The English people welcomed my battalion with open arms. The color of my skin was irrevelant, and I was looked upon as merely an American soldier. I walked in the streets, attended dances, went to the theater, and sat wherever I wanted. I was a free man. I was very happy when my captain reluctantly told me that both of us had been invited to dinner by the same British family. It was as if I had found beauty and calmness,

because of the English people. Once more I could have faith in my fellow human beings.

Time moves on and seasons change, and so it was with me as I crossed the English Channel to France, where the horrors of war became real to me. I saw my friends and many men of my battalion dying. I fought with the thought in mind that the Germans were our enemy, not really having any idea of Hitler's philosophy.

My unit became involved in the Battle of the Bulge. We built bridges so that American units could go and attack the Germans at Bastogne. Later, I was one of the American soldiers who liberated Buchenwald, one of the largest concentration camps in Germany.

Buchenwald

As I walked through the gates of the concentration camp, totally unaware of what I was going to see and not knowing what to expect, coming towards me were what re-

A segregated water fountain.

sembled people. I stopped and stared, not believing what I saw. Blinking my eyes, I saw before me what looked like a group of skeletons. All of them looked the same — skin and bones. I took in a deep breath and decided to find out who these people were and what had happened to them. Determined, I found a person who could communicate with me, who took me from place to place within the camp. As we walked he told me that the Nazis brought people to this camp whom they considered "undesirables." A very large majority of them were Jews. A small percentage was made up of Gypsies, Communists, and handicapped people. The only crime these people had committed were that they had been born Jews, Gypsies, handicapped.

Arriving at plain wooden barracks, I entered one, seeing nothing but toilets where people had to sit together, without any privacy. In another building was a crematorium. Inside there were the ovens, full of ashes. Walking as if in a fog, I wondered, "Where are the old people and the children?" The answer was that they had already been exterminated. What appeared to be another skeleton sitting on the ground was a human being trying to raise himself. I approached him, asking, "Where is your family?" He answered, "None is left, and if you hadn't come now, I too would be dead in a few days." But he continued, "If I die now I don't mind, because I will die as a free man."

Jewish children. Victims of the "final solution" begging for a crust of bread.

What kinds of human beings did such things? It was the SS, trained to believe that only the German Aryan race had the right to live. These SS, who loved their own children, somehow could not hear the cries of other children. They claimed to love music but could not hear the sad melodies of the innocent children. These SS or Gestapo could see leaves falling from the trees but would not see the collapsing bodies. What kind of people were they? Hitler alone could not have done this. His evil plan was carried out by people who claimed to follow their religions, and said that they believe in God, but did not understand the meaning of the Ten Commandments. Teenagers who followed their leaders blindly. Millions of people who were quiet, saying not a word. They were janitors, truck drivers, doctors, housewives, and lawyers. People who could not and would not think for themselves. People who chose to ignore the values of man and the true meaning of life.

The people killed by Hitler and his SS never had a chance to fulfill their dreams. They were musicians, inventors, scientists, mothers and fathers. Their children, who could have created a better world, died because some of their friends and others stood by and did nothing. Because of this, the brutality of anti-Semitism, bigotry, and racism put an end to whatever future they might have had.

With outstretched hands, people asked for food, and as much as we would have liked to feed them, we were not allowed to do so. Due to their weakened condition, their stomachs could not handle solid food at this time. I wondered how these weakened, hungry people could have survived the bitter winters and the intense heat of the summers, wearing only short, striped shirts and ragged torn pants.

Sickened inside the camp, I left trembling as I did so. Outside the camp were the most beautiful homes I had ever seen. Shining on the green June grass was the warm sun. It

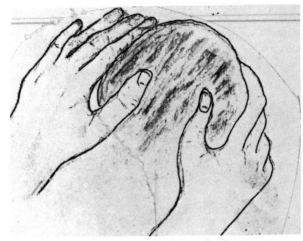

was hard to conceive that anything I had just seen could have happened in this environment. There were no people to be seen. The only sound you could hear was the chirping of a bird. Within the houses were the people who had ignored the smell of the ovens and the screams for help, afraid and wondering what would become of them. Slowly they walked out of their homes, staring at us. I asked a few if they knew what had happened here in their neighborhood. They denied knowing anything. We took these people, men, women, and children, through the gates of Buchenwald, showing them the inhumanity of man to man. There were many who just closed their eyes, some who broke down and cried, and a few who were in a state of shock.

The German people, who had given the world so many great musicians, writers, and scientists, were taught to believe that the Jewish people were the cause of their problems. German youngsters were taught that Deutschland would have everything if it only got rid of its Jews. They were instilled with hatred, and they preached to the world, by example, what they believed. Now they could see what their preaching had accomplished.

I knew how important it was for people to see and understand what hatred could do, and I hoped and prayed that this genocide, this Holocaust, would be a very meaningful lesson learned by all of us; and that is why, dear children, I am telling you this story.

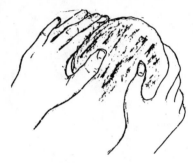

A Black Soldier

Something to Think About

This chapter is the story of a non-Jewish soldier. It gives us the opportunity to ask what Jewish tradition says about gentiles. Is there a Jewish attitude towards non-Jews? Actually, the answer to this question has differed in different times and places. But in general we can say that the Jewish attitude towards gentiles is largely the result of gentile attitudes towards Jews. In times when gentiles showed friendship toward Jews, Jews displayed warm feelings in return.

Voices from Tradition

Rabbi Jeremiah said: "How can you know that a gentile who practices the Law is equal to the high priest? Because it says, 'Which if a man do, he shall live through them' (Leviticus 18:5). And it says, 'This is the Law (Torah) of man' (II Samuel 7:19). It does not say: 'The Law of priest, Levites, Israelites,' but, 'This is the Law of man, O Lord God.' And it does not say, 'Open the gates, and let the priests and Levites and Israel enter,' but it says, 'Open the gates that a righteous gentile may enter' (Isaiah 26:2); and it says, 'This is the gate of the Lord, the righteous shall enter it.' It does not say, 'The priests and the Levites and Israel shall enter it,' but it says, 'The righteous shall enter it' (Psalms 118:20). And it does not say, 'Do good, O Lord, to the priests and the Levites and the Israelites,' but it says, 'Do good, O Lord, to the good' (Psalms 125:4). So even a gentile, if he practices the Law, is equal to the high priest.

— Sifra 86b

Joshua ben Hananiah said that the righteous of all nations have a share in the world-to-come.

— Tosefta (Sanhedrin 13:2)

And in Your Opinion...

1. We learn a lot about Leon Bass's background. Do you think his special background made a difference in his later experience at Buchenwald?

2. If you think it did, what specifically made the difference?

3. Leon Bass tells us after his experience at Buchenwald that "Hitler alone could not have done this. It was people who claimed to follow their religions, who said that they believed in God but did not understand the meaning of the Ten Commandments." What did he mean?

4. Above are two passages from our tradition. How would you apply them to Leon Bass? How would you apply them to the Nazis?